THE MOVING PICTURE GIRLS AT ROCKY RANCH

Or, Great Days Among the Cowboys

LAURA LEE HOPE

1st WORLD
LIBRARY
Literary Society

The Moving Picture Girls at Rocky Ranch

Laura Lee Hope

© 1st World Library, 2007
PO Box 2211
Fairfield, IA 52556
www.1stworldlibrary.com
First Edition

LCCN: 2007934154

Softcover ISBN: 978-1-4218-9657-1
Hardcover ISBN: 978-1-4218-9757-8
eBook ISBN: 978-1-4218-9557-4

Purchase *"The Moving Picture Girls at Rocky Ranch"*
as a traditional bound book at:
www.1stWorldLibrary.com/purchase.asp?ISBN=978-1-4218-9657-1

1st World Library is a literary, educational organization
dedicated to:

- Creating a free internet library of downloadable ebooks

- Hosting writing competitions and offering book publishing
scholarships.

Interested in more 1st World Library books? contact:
literacy@1stworldlibrary.com
Check us out at: www.1stworldlibrary.com

1ˢᵗ World Library Literary Society

Giving Back to the World

"If you want to work on the core problem, it's early school literacy."

- James Barksdale, former CEO of Netscape

"No skill is more crucial to the future of a child, or to a democratic and prosperous society, than literacy."

- Los Angeles Times

"Literacy... means far more than learning how to read and write... The aim is to transmit... knowledge and promote social participation."

- UNESCO

"Literacy is not a luxury, it is a right and a responsibility. If our world is to meet the challenges of the twenty-first century we must harness the energy and creativity of all our citizens."

- President Bill Clinton

"Parents should be encouraged to read to their children, and teachers should be equipped with all available techniques for teaching literacy, so the varying needs and capacities of individual kids can be taken into account."

- Hugh Mackay

CONTENTS

CHAPTER I

THE SPY

"Well, Ruth, aren't you almost ready?"

"Just a moment, Alice. I can't seem to get my collar fastened in the back. I wish I'd used the old-fashioned hooks and eyes instead of those new snaps."

"Oh, I think those snaps are just adorable!"

"Oh, Alice DeVere! Using such an extreme expression!"

"What expression, Ruth?"

"'Adorable!' You sometimes accuse me of using slang, and there you go—"

"'Adorable' isn't slang," retorted Alice.

"Oh, isn't it though? Since when?"

"There you go yourself! You're as bad as I am."

"Well, it must be associating with you, then," sighed Ruth.

"No, Ruth, it's this moving picture business. It just makes you use words that *mean* something, and not those that are merely sign-posts. I'm glad to see that you are getting— sensible. But never mind about that. Are you ready to go to the studio? I'm sure we'll be late."

"Oh, please help me with this collar. I wish I'd made this waist with the new low-cut effect. Not too low, of course," Ruth added hastily, as she caught a surprised glance from her sister.

Two girls were in a room about which were strewn many articles of feminine adornment. Yet it was not an untidy apartment. True, dresser drawers did yawn and disclose their contents, and closet doors gaped at one, showing a collection of shoes and skirts. But then the occupants of the room might have been forgiven, for they were in haste to keep an appointment.

"There, Ruth," finally exclaimed the younger of the two girls—yet she was not so much younger—not more than two years. "I think your collar is perfectly sweet."

"It's good of you to say so. You know I got it at that little French shop around the corner, but sewed some of that Mexican drawn lace on to make it a bit higher. Now I'm sorry I did, for I had to put in those snap fasteners instead of hooks. And if you don't get them to fit exactly they come loose. It's like when the film doesn't come right on the screen, and the piano player sounds a discord to call the operator's attention to it."

"You've hit it, sister mine."

"Oh, Alice! There you go again. 'Hit it!'"

Laura Lee Hope

"You'd say 'hit it' at a baseball game," Alice retorted.

"Oh, yes, I suppose so. But we're not at one," objected the older girl, as she finished buttoning her gloves, and took up her parasol, which she shook out, to make sure that it would open easily when needed.

"There, I think I'm ready," announced Alice, as she slipped on a light jacket, for, though it was spring, the two rivers of New York sent rather chilling breezes across the city, and a light waist was rather conducive to colds.

"Have you the key?" asked the older girl, as she paused for a moment on the threshold of the private hall of the apartment house. She had tied her veil rather tightly at the back, knotting it and fastening it with a little gold pin, and now she pulled it away from her cheeks, to relieve the tension.

"Yes, I have it, Ruth. Oh, don't make such funny faces! Anyone would think you were posing."

"Well, I'm not—but this veil—tickles."

"Serves you right for trying to be so stylish."

"It's proper to have a certain amount of style, Alice, dear. I wish I could induce you to have more of it."

"I have enough, thank you. Let's don't talk dress any more, or we'll have a tiff before we get to the moving picture studio, and there are some long and trying scenes ahead of us to-day."

"So there are. I wonder if daddy took his key?"

"Wait, and I'll look on his dresser."

The younger girl went back into the apartment for a moment, while her sister stepped across the corridor and tapped lightly at an opposite door.

"Has Russ gone?" she asked the pleasant-faced woman who answered.

"Yes, Ruth. A little while ago. He was going to call for you girls, but I knew you were dressing, for Alice came in to borrow some pins, so I told him not to wait."

"That's right. We'll see him at the studio."

"You're coming in to supper to-night, you know."

"Oh, yes, Mrs. Dalwood. Daddy wouldn't miss that for anything!" laughed Ruth, as she turned to wait for her sister. "Of course he *says* our cooking is the best he ever had since poor mamma left us," Ruth went on, "but I just *know* he relishes yours a great deal more."

"Oh, you're just saying that, Ruth!" objected the neighbor.

"Indeed I'm not. You should hear him talk, for days afterward, about your clam chowder." She laughed genially.

"Well, he does seem to relish that," admitted Mrs. Dalwood.

"What's that?" asked Alice, as she came out.

"We're speaking of clam chowder, and how fond daddy is of Mrs. Dalwood's recipe," said Ruth.

"Oh, yes, indeed! I should think he'd be ashamed to look a clam in the face—that is, if a clam *has* a face," laughed Alice. "It's awfully good of you, Mrs. Dalwood, to make it for him so often."

"Well, I'm always glad when a man enjoys his meals," declared Mrs. Dalwood, who, being a widow, knew what the lack of proper home life meant.

"I'm afraid we're imposing on you," suggested Alice, as she started down the stairs. "You have us over to tea so often, and we seldom invite you."

"Now don't be thinking that, my dear!" exclaimed the neighbor. "I know what it is when you have to pose so much for moving pictures.

"My boy Russ tells me what long hours you put in, and how hard you work. And it's trouble enough to get up a meal these days, and have anything left to pay the rent. So I'm only too glad when you can come in and enjoy the victuals with us. I cook too much anyhow, and of late Russ seems to have lost his appetite."

"I fancy I know why," laughed Alice, with a roguish glance at her sister.

"Alice!" protested Ruth, in shocked tones. "Don't you dare—"

"I was only going to say that he has not seemed well since coming back from Florida—what was the harm in that?" Alice wanted to know.

"Oh!" murmured Ruth. "Do come on," she added, as if she feared her fun-loving sister might say something embarrassing.

"Russ will be better soon, Mrs. Dalwood," Alice called as

she and her sister went down the stairway of the apartment house.

"What makes you think so?" asked his mother. "Not but what I'm glad to hear you say that, for really he hasn't eaten at all well lately."

"We're going on the road again, I hear," went on Alice. "The whole moving picture company is to be taken off somewhere, and a lot of films made. Russ always likes that, and I'm sure his appetite will come back as soon as we start traveling. It always does."

"You are getting to be a close observer," remarked Ruth, with just the hint of sarcasm in her voice. "Oh, Alice, do finish buttoning your gloves in the house!" she exclaimed. "It looks so careless to go out fussing with them."

"All right, sister mine. Anything to keep peace in the family!" laughed the younger girl.

Together they went down the street, a charming picture of youth and happiness.

A little later they entered the studio of the Comet Film Company, a concern engaged in the business of making moving pictures, from posing them with actors and actresses, and the suitable "properties," to the leasing of the completed films to the various theaters throughout the country.

Alice and Ruth DeVere, of whom you will hear more later, with their father, were engaged in this work, and very interesting and profitable they found it.

As the girls entered the studio they were greeted by a number of other players, and an elderly gentleman, with a bearing and carriage that revealed the schooling of many years behind the footlights, came forward.

"I was just wondering where you were," he said with a smile. His voice was husky and hoarse, and indicated that he had some throat affection. In fact, that same throat trouble was the cause of Hosmer DeVere being in moving picture work instead of in the legitimate drama, in which he had formerly been a leading player.

"We stopped a moment to speak to Mrs. Dalwood," explained Ruth.

"Clam chowder," added Alice, with a laugh. "She's going to have it this evening, Daddy."

"Good!" he exclaimed, rubbing his hands together in a manner that indicated gratification. "I was just hungry for some."

"You always seem able to eat that," laughed Alice. "I must learn how to make it."

"I wish you would!" exclaimed her father, earnestly. "Then when we are on the road I can have some, now and then."

"Oh, you are hopeless!" laughed Alice. "Here is your latch-key, Daddy," she went on, handing it to him. "You left it on your dresser, and as Ruth and I are going shopping when we get through here, I thought you might want it."

"Thank you, I probably shall. I am going home from here to study a new part."

The scene in the studio of the moving picture concern was a lively one. Men were moving about whole "rooms"—or, at least they appeared as such on the film. Others were setting various parts of the stage, electricians were adjusting the powerful lights, cameras were being set up on their tripods, and operators were at the handles, grinding away, for several plays were being made at once.

"Just in time, Ruth and Alice!" called Russ Dalwood, who was one of the chief camera men. "Your scene goes on in ten minutes. You have just time to dress."

"It's that 'Quaker Maid;' isn't it?" asked Ruth, for she and her sisters took part in so many plays that often it was hard to remember which particular one was to be filmed.

"That's it," said Russ. "Don't forget your bonnets!" he laughed as he focused the camera.

"All ready now!" called Mr. Pertell, the manager of the company, and also the chief stage director, a little later. "Take your places, if you please! Mr. DeVere, you are not in this until the second scene. Mr. Bunn, you'll not need your high hat in this act."

"But I thought you said—" began an elderly actor, of the type known as "Hams," from their insatiable desire to portray the character of Hamlet.

"I know I did," said Mr. Pertell, sharply. "But I have had to change my mind. You are to take the part of a plumber, and you come to fix a burst water pipe. So get your overalls and your kit. You have a plumber's kit; haven't you, Pop?" the manager called to Pop Snooks, the property man, who was obliged, on short notice, to provide anything from a diamond ring to a rustic bridge.

"All right for the plumber!" called Pop. "Have it for you in

14   Laura Lee Hope

a minute."

"And, Mr. Sneed," called the manager to another actor. "You are supposed to be the householder whose water pipe has burst. You try to putty it up and you get soaked. Go over there in the far corner, where the tank is; we don't want water running into this Quaker scene."

"Oh, I get all wet; do I?" asked Mr. Sneed, in no very pleasant tones.

"That's what you do!"

"Well, all I've got to say is that I wish you'd give some of these tank dramas to someone else. I'm getting tired of being soaked."

"You haven't been really wet since the trip to Florida," declared Mr. Pertell. "Lively now, we have no time to lose. Come on, Russ!" he called to the young operator. "You're to film the Quaker scenario. I'll have Johnson make the water pipe scene. All ready, ladies and gentlemen!"

Various plays were going on at once in different parts of the studio. Ruth and Alice DeVere took their places in one where a Quaker story was being portrayed. Later they posed in a church scene, in which a number of extra people, or "supers," were engaged to represent the congregation.

Mr. Pertell, once he had the various scenes going, took a moment in which to rest, for he was a very busy man. He sat down near Alice, who, for the time being, was out of the scene. But hardly had the manager stretched out in a chair, resting one shirt-sleeved arm over the back, when he started up, and looked intently toward one corner of the studio.

"I wonder why he is going in there?" observed the manager, half aloud.

"Who?" asked Alice, for the moving picture company was like one big family, in a way.

"That new man," went on Mr. Pertell. "Harry Wilson, he said his name was. Now he's going into the proof room, where he has no business. I must look into this. I wonder, after all, if there could be any truth in that warning I received the other day."

"What warning?" asked Alice.

"About a rival film company trying to discover some of the secrets of our success. I must look into this."

He sprang from his chair and hurried across the big studio toward the room where the films were first shown privately, to correct any defects, mechanical or artistic. It was there that the initial performance, so to speak, was given.

Before Mr. Pertell reached the room, where the projection machine was installed, the man of whom he had spoken had entered. And, just as the manager reached the door, the same man came violently out, impelled by a vigorous push from one of the operators, who at the same time cried:

"Get out of here, you spy! What do you mean by sneaking in here, trying to get our secrets? Get out! Where's Mr. Pertell? I'll tell him about you."

Laura Lee Hope

CHAPTER II

WESTERN PLANS

"What is it, Walsh? What is the trouble?" exclaimed Mr. Pertell, as he hastened toward the proving room, where the films were tested before being "released."

"This man, Mr. Pertell! This fellow you hired as a comedy actor. He came in here just now, and I caught him starting to take notes of the first film of our new play."

"You did!" cried the manager sharply.

"Yes. He came in when it was dark; but the film broke, and I turned on the light. Then I caught him!"

"That's not so—you did not!"

The accused man—the spy he had been called—stood facing them all, the picture of injured innocence. Ruth, Alice and some of the other women members of the company drew aside, a little frightened at the prospect of trouble.

And trouble seemed imminent, for it was easy to see that Mr. Pertell was very angry. As for the other, his face was white with either anger or fear—perhaps the latter.

"I saw you taking notes of the action on that film!" cried James Walsh, the testing room expert.

"And I say you did not!" asserted Harry Wilson, the new player, hired a few days before as a "comic relief." The other members of the company knew very little of him, and he had attracted small attention until this episode. During a period when he was not engaged in one of the plays he had gone into the room, permission to enter which was not often granted, even to favored members of the Comet Film concern—at least until after the release of the film was decided.

"Don't let that man get way!" cried Mr. Pertell, sharply, as he saw Wilson edging toward the hallway. "Lock the doors and we'll search him!"

There was some confusion for a moment, but the doors were locked, and Pop Snooks seized the new actor.

And, while preparations are being made to search the man I will trespass on the time of my new readers sufficiently to tell them, as briefly as I can, something about the previous books of this series, and of the main characters in this one.

The initial volume was entitled "The Moving Picture Girls; Or, First Appearances in Photo Dramas." The girls were Ruth and Alice DeVere, aged respectively seventeen and fifteen years. Their mother was dead, and they lived with their father, Hosmer DeVere, in the Fenmore Apartment House, New York. Across the hall from them lived Russ Dalwood, a moving picture operator, with his widowed mother, and his brother Billy.

Mr. DeVere was a talented actor in the "legitimate," as it is called to distinguish it from vaudeville and moving pictures.

But the recurrence of an old throat ailment made him suddenly so hoarse that he could not speak loud enough to be heard across the footlights. He was already rehearsing for a new play when this happened, and after several trials to make himself audible, he was finally forced to give up his engagement.

This was doubly hard, as the DeVeres were in straitened circumstances at this time, money being very scarce. They had really entered upon a period of "hard times" when Russ, a manly young fellow, whose first acquaintance with the girls had quickly ripened into friendship, made a suggestion.

"Why don't you try moving pictures?" he had said to Mr. DeVere. "You can act, all right, and you won't have to use your voice."

At first the veteran actor was much opposed to to the idea, rather looking down upon moving pictures as "common." But his daughters induced him to try it, and he came to like them very much. The pay, too, was good.

Thus Mr. DeVere became attached to the Comet Film Company. Mr. Frank Pertell, as I have said, was manager, and Russ was his chief operator, though there were several others. There were, too, a number of actors and actresses attached to the company. Besides Ruth, Alice and their father, there were Miss Laura Dixon and Miss Pearl Pennington, former vaudeville stars, between whom and the DeVere girls there was not the best of feeling. Ruth and Alice thought that the two actresses were of a rather too "showy" type, and Miss Pennington and Miss Dixon rather looked down on Alice and Ruth as being "slow" and old-fashioned.

Pop Snooks, as I have intimated, was the efficient property

man. Paul Ardite, whom Alice liked very much, was the juvenile leading man.

Wellington Bunn was the "old school" actor already mentioned. He and Pepper Sneed were rather alike in one way—they made many objections when called on to do "stunts" out of the ordinary. Mr. Bunn always wanted to play Shakespearean parts, and Mr. Sneed was always fearful that something was going to happen.

Of a contrasting disposition was Carl Switzer, the jolly German comedian. Nothing came amiss to him, and he was always ready for whatever was on the program, making a joke of even hard and dangerous work.

Mrs. Maguire was the "mother" of the company. She often played "old woman" parts, and her two grandchildren, Tommy and Nellie, were sometimes used in child sketches.

Ruth and Alice really got into moving picture work by accident. One day two extra actresses failed to appear when needed, and Mr. Pertell, who was in a hurry, appealed to Mr. DeVere to allow his daughters to "fill in." They did so well that they were engaged permanently, and very much did they like their work.

Alice was like her dead mother, happy, full of life and jollity, and her brown eyes generally sparkled with laughter. She was a rather matter-of-fact nature, whereas Ruth was more romantic. Ruth was a deal like her father, inclined to look on the more serious side of life. But her blue eyes could be laughing and jolly, too, and between the two girls there was really not so much difference after all.

Soon after getting into moving picture work they became aware of a bold attempt to get away from Russ Dalwood an invention he had made for a camera. How Ruth and Alice frustrated this, and how they "made good," as Mr. Pertell put it, in an important drama, is fully told in the first book.

The second volume was entitled "The Moving Picture Girls at Oak Farm; Or, Queer Happenings While Taking Rural Plays." The manager had made the acquaintance of Sandy Apgar in New York. Sandy managed his father's farm, in New Jersey, and Mr. Pertell took his entire company there, to make a series of farm dramas.

A curious mystery developed at once, and did not end until the discovery of a certain secret room, in which was concealed a treasure that was of the utmost benefit to the Apgar family.

"The Moving Picture Girls Snowbound; Or, The Proof on the Film," was the third book. To get a series of dramas in which snow and ice effects would form the background, Mr. Pertell took his company of players to the backwoods of New England. There they had rather more snow than they expected, and were caught in a blizzard.

Also Ruth and Alice made a curious discovery concerning a dishonest man, and not only frustrated his plans to swindle a certain company, but also were able to save their father from paying a debt the second time. In addition they took part in many important plays.

From the cold bleakness of New England to the balmy air of Florida was a change that Ruth and Alice experienced later, for on their return to New York from the backwoods the members of the company were sent to the peninsular state.

In "The Moving Picture Girls Under the Palms; Or, Lost in the Wilds of Florida," is related what happened when the company went South.

Exciting incidents occurred from the first, when the ship caught fire, and, even as it burned, Russ "filmed" it.

But the company reached St. Augustine safely, and then came busy times, making various moving picture dramas.

How the two sisters learned of the plight of the two girls whom they knew slightly, and how after getting lost themselves on one of the sluggish rivers of interior Florida, Ruth and Alice were able to render a great service to the Madison girls—this you may read in the fourth volume.

The company had come back to New York in the spring, and now nearly all the members were assembled at the studio, when the incident narrated in the first chapter took place.

"Here it is!" cried Mr. Pertell, as, slipping his hand into the pocket of the accused actor, he brought forth a crumpled paper.

"And wasn't he making notes, just as I said, of our new big play?" demanded Walsh.

"That's what he was!" exclaimed the manager as he quickly scanned the crumpled document. "He didn't have time to make many notes, though."

"No, I was too quick for him!" declared the tester.

Harry Wilson had no more to say. His bravado deserted him and he was now in abject fear.

"What have you to say for yourself?" demanded Mr. Pertell, angrily.

Laura Lee Hope

The other did not answer.

"Now, you get out of here!" ordered the manager, "and never come back."

"I'll not go until I get what is coming to me," was the sullen retort.

"If you got what is coming to you it would be arrest!" declared Walsh.

"I want my money!" mumbled Wilson.

"Here is an order on the cashier for it," said Mr. Pertell. "Get it and—go!"

Hastily writing on a slip of paper, he tendered it to the actor, who took it without a word, and slunk off. The others watched him curiously. It was something they had never before witnessed—an attempt to gain possession of the secrets of the company—for a moving picture concern guards its films jealously, until they are "released," or ready for reproduction.

"Curious," remarked Mr. Pertell, "but I had a distrust of that chap from the first. Do any of you know him?"

"I acted mit him vunce in der Universal company, but he dit not stay long," said Mr. Switzer.

"Probably he was up to some underhand work," observed Walsh.

"I wonder what his object was?" went on the manager. "He evidently wasn't doing this for himself." Idly he turned over the scrap of paper on which the other had been making notes in the testing room. Then the manager uttered a cry of surprise.

"Ha! The International Picture Company! This is part of one of their letter heads. So Wilson was working for them! They very likely sent him here to get a position, and instructed him to steal some of our secrets and ideas, if he could. The scoundrel!"

"He didn't see much!" chuckled Walsh. "The film broke after a few feet had been run off, and I switched on the lights. He didn't see a great deal."

"No, his notes show that," said the manager. "But only for that accident he might have learned of our plans and given our rivals information sufficient to spoil our big play."

"Have you new plans?" asked Mr. DeVere, who was on very friendly terms with the manager.

"Yes, we are going to make a big three-reel play, called 'East and West,' and while some of the scenes will be laid in New York, the main ones will be filmed out beyond the Mississippi. One of the most important New York scenes has already been made. It was this one which was being tested when Wilson went in there. Had he seen it all he might have guessed at the rest of our plans and our rivals, the International people, would have been able to get ahead of us. They are always on the alert to take the ideas of other concerns. But I think I'll beat them this time."

"So we are to go West; eh?" queried Mr. DeVere.

"Yes, out on what prairies are left, in some rather wild sections, and I think we will make the best views we have yet had," responded Mr. Pertell. "Now, if you please, ladies and gentlemen, take your places, and go on with your acts. I am sorry this interruption distracted you."

CHAPTER III

A DARING FEAT

"Oh, Ruth, did you hear? We are to go out West!"

"Are you glad, Alice?"

"Indeed I am. Why, we can see Indians and cowboys, and ride bucking broncos and all that. Oh, it's perfectly delightful!" and Alice, who had been taking down her jacket, held it in her arms, as one might clasp a dancing partner, and swept about the now almost deserted studio in a hesitation waltz.

"Can't I come in on that?" cried Paul Ardite, as he began to whistle, keeping time with Alice's steps.

"No, indeed, I'm too tired," she answered, with a laugh. "Oh, but to think of going West! I've always wanted to!"

"Alice always says that, whenever a new location is decided on," observed Ruth, with a quiet smile.

The work of the day was over, and most of the players had gone home. Ruth and Alice were waiting for their father, who was in Mr. Pertell's office. They had intended going shopping, thinking Mr. De Vere would be detained, but he

Laura Lee Hope

had said he would be with them directly.

And the two girls had brought up the subject of the new line of work, broached by Mr. Pertell in mentioning the matter of the spy.

"I hope nothing comes of that incident," said Mr. DeVere, as he came from the manager's office, while Ruth and Alice finished their preparations for the street.

"I hope not, either," returned the manager, slipping into his coat, for, like many busy men, he worked best in his shirt sleeves. "Yet I don't like it, and I am frank to confess that the International concern has more than once tried to get the best of me by underhand work. I don't like it. I must keep track of that Wilson. Good night, ladies. Good night, Mr. DeVere."

The good nights were returned and then the two girls, with their father, Russ and Paul, went out.

"That was an unfortunate occurrence," remarked Mr. DeVere.

"Oh, Daddy! How hoarse you are!" exclaimed Ruth, laying a daintily-gloved hand on his shoulder. "You must use your throat spray as soon as you get home."

"I will. My throat is a little raw. There was considerable dust in the studio to-day. I like work in the open air best."

"So do I," confessed Alice. "Now, Daddy, you must stop talking," and she shook her finger at him. "You listen—we'll talk."

"You mean *you* will," laughed Ruth, for Alice generally did her own, and part of Ruth's share also.

They walked on, talking at intervals of the incident of the spy and again of the prospective trip to the West.

"Do you know just where we are going, Russ?" asked Ruth, as she kept pace with him.

"Not exactly," he replied, stealing a glance at the girl beside him, for she was a picture fair to look upon with her almost golden hair blown about her face by the light breeze, while her blue eyes looked into the more sober gray ones of Russ. "I believe Mr. Pertell intends to go to several places, so as to get varied views. I know we are to go to a ranch, for one thing."

"Fine!" exclaimed Alice, with almost boyish enthusiasm, as she walked at the side of Paul. "Daddy, do you want me to become a cowgirl?" she asked, turning to Mr. DeVere, who was in the rear.

"I guess if you wanted to be one, you would whether I wanted you to or not," he replied, with an indulgent smile. "You have a way with you!"

"Hasn't she, though!" agreed Paul.

They reached the apartment house where the DeVeres and Russ lived. Paul came in for a little while, but declined an invitation to stay to tea.

"I've got quite a piece of work on for to-morrow," he said, as he left.

"What is it?" asked Alice.

"There's to be a new play, 'An Inventor's Troubles,' and one of the inventions is a sort of rope fire escape. There's a rope, coiled in a metal case. You take it to your hotel room with you, and in case of fire you fasten the case to the window casing, grab one end of the rope, and jump. The rope is supposed to pay out slowly, by means of friction pulleys, and you come safely to the ground."

"Did you invent that?" asked Ruth, who had not heard all that was said.

"Oh, no, some fellow did, and the city authorities are going to give him a chance to demonstrate it before they will recommend it to hotel proprietors. And I'm to be the 'goat,' if you will allow me to say so."

"How?" asked Alice.

"I'm to come down on the rope from the tenth story of some building. This will serve as the city test, and at the same time Mr. Pertell has fixed up a story in which the fire escape scene figures. I've got to study up a little bit before to-morrow."

"It—it isn't dangerous; is it?" asked Alice, and she rather faltered over the words.

"Not if the thing works," replied Paul, with a shrug of his shoulders. "That is, if the rope doesn't break, or pay out so fast that I hit the pavement with a bump."

"Oh, is it as dangerous as that?" exclaimed Alice, looking at Paul intently.

"Don't worry," and he smiled. "I guess the apparatus has been tested before. I'm getting used to risks in this business."

"What time to-morrow is it?" queried Ruth.

"Right after lunch," Russ responded. "I've got to film him."

"Then I'm coming to see you!" declared Alice. "I'm off directly after lunch. I haven't much on for to-morrow."

"Oh, Alice! You wouldn't go!" cried her sister.

"Of course I would, my dear!"

"But suppose something—happened?" Ruth went on in a low voice, as Russ and Paul started out together.

"All the more reason why I should be there!" declared Alice, promptly, and Ruth looked at her with a new light of understanding in her eyes. And then she looked at Paul, who waved his hand gaily at the younger girl.

"Dear little sister," murmured Ruth. "I wonder—?"

"I'll look for you there," called Paul, as he went on down the hall.

"And I'll be there," promised Alice.

"Do you feel better now, Daddy?" asked Ruth, in their rooms.

"Much better—yes, my dear. That new spray the doctor gave me seems to work wonders. And my throat is really better since our trip South. I feel quite encouraged."

It was after supper in the DeVere apartment. The two girls were seated at the sitting-room table with their father, who was looking over a new play in which he had a part. Alice was reading a newspaper and Ruth mending a pair of stockings.

Laura Lee Hope

"Well, there's one good thing about going out West," finally remarked the younger girl, as she tossed aside the paper, and caught up a hairpin which her vigorous motion had caused to slip out of her brown tresses.

"What's that—you won't have to fuss so about dress?" asked Ruth, for her sister did not share her ideas on this subject.

"No, but if we do go there won't be any trouble about that International company trying to steal Mr. Pertell's secrets."

"I don't know about that," observed Mr. DeVere, slowly. "If they are after his big drama they may even follow us out West."

"Oh, I hope not!" exclaimed Ruth, pausing with extended needle. "I don't like trouble."

"There may be no trouble," her father assured her, with a smile. "In fact, now that the spy is detected, the whole affair may be closed. I hope so, for Mr. Pertell works hard to get up new ideas, and to have some other concern step in, and rob him of the fruits of his labor, would be unjust indeed."

Rehearsals and the filming of plays in the Comet studio were over the next morning about eleven o'clock.

"Come on," said Paul to Ruth and Alice. "I'm to get a bonus on account of the fire escape stunt, and I'll take you girls out to lunch. Come along, Russ. It's extra money and we might as well enjoy it."

"You are too extravagant!" chided Ruth.

"Oh, I like to be—when I have the chance," Paul laughed. "It isn't often I do."

"Well, then, we may as well help you out," agreed Russ. "Right after lunch we'll give you a chance to show us what you can do on that patent rope."

The little meal was a merry one, in spite of the fact that the two girls were a little nervous about going to see Paul descend from the tenth story of a building on a slender rope. Ruth had finally consented to accompany her sister.

Together they went to the place where the test was to take place. It was a tall office structure, and, as word of what was afoot had spread, quite a throng had gathered.

Mr. Pertell had made arrangements with the authorities to have Paul work in a little theatrical business in connection with the test, and the inventor of the fire escape was also to be in the moving pictures.

There was a little preliminary scene, as part of the projected play, and then Paul went into the building with the inventor to prepare for his thrilling descent.

The apparatus seemed simple. It was a round, metallic case, inside of which was coiled a stout rope. At the end was a broad leather strap, intended to be fastened about the person who was to make the jump. The case, and the coil of rope, were to be fastened to a hook at the side of the window. Then Paul was to jump out, and trust to the slow uncoiling of the rope to lower him safely.

"Are you all ready?" asked the inventor, after he had explained the apparatus.

"As ready as I ever shall be," answered Paul a little nervously. He looked down to the ground. It seemed a long way off.

CHAPTER IV

A CLOUD OF SMOKE

Below, in the crowd that had gathered to watch the test, were Ruth and Alice. Russ, of course, was there with his moving picture camera, and Paul saw the little lens-tube aimed in his direction, like the muzzle of some new weapon.

"Now, don't get nervous," directed the inventor, after he had explained the mechanism to Paul, and also to the city officials who had gathered to pass upon its merits.

"You can't make me nervous," declared the young actor. "I've gone through too much in this moving picture business, though I will admit I never jumped from such a height before."

"Don't look down," the inventor warned him. "You won't get dizzy then. And don't think of the height. With this apparatus it is impossible to get hurt. You will go down like a feather."

"That's comforting to know," laughed Paul. "Well, I may as well start, I guess."

The belt was adjusted about him, and as it was done in the open window Russ was able to get views of it, and of all that went on. Then Paul got out on the sill. There he paused a moment.

"I—I can't bear to look at him!" murmured Ruth.

"Don't be silly," exclaimed Alice.

"But suppose—suppose something happens?"

"Don't be a Mr. Sneed!" retorted her sister, with a laugh. "I don't believe anything will happen, and if—if he should fall —see!" and she pointed to where a detachment of city firemen stood ready with their life net.

"Oh, I didn't notice them before," confessed Ruth. "That makes it safer."

"All ready down there, Russ?" shouted Paul, through a megaphone. "Shall I go?"

"Jump! I'm all ready for you," was the answer.

Paul paused but for a moment, and then he jumped from the sill, and out away from the building. The coil of rope in the metal case had been swung out from the side of the structure on an arm, so as to enable Paul to clear the lower window ledges.

For the first few feet he went down like a shot, and for one horrible moment he felt that something had gone wrong. In fact the crowd did also, for there was a hoarse shout of alarm.

"Oh!" gasped Ruth, faintly.

"I—I—" began Alice, as she, too, turned aside her head.

Then someone yelled:

"It's all right!"

Alice looked then.

She saw Paul descending as the rope payed out. He was coming down gradually.

"That will make a good film," commented Russ to Mr. Pertell, for the manager had come to witness the fire escape scene.

"Indeed it will."

Paul came down several stories, and the success of the apparatus seemed assured when, at about the fourth story from the ground, something suddenly went wrong.

Once more the young actor shot downward and this time it seemed that he would be seriously injured.

Russ felt that he must rush forward to save his friend, but he had an inborn instinct to stick to his camera—an instinct that probably every moving picture operator has, even though he does violence to his own feelings.

"He'll be hurt!" several in the crowd cried.

Ruth and Alice both turned aside their heads again, but there was no need for alarm.

For the firemen, at the word of command from their captain, had rushed forward with the life net. They were standing only a few feet away from where Paul dangled in the air, but even at that they were only just in time.

Paul fell into it heavily, for the mechanism depended on to check the speed at which the rope payed out, did not work. But the firemen knew just how to handle a situation of that sort, and they held firmly to the net. It sagged under the impact of Paul's body, but he bounded upward again in an instant, and then was helped out of the net and to his feet.

"Mighty lucky you fellows were here," observed the young actor, as the cheers of the crowd died down.

"I was afraid something like that might happen," spoke the fire captain. "I've seen too many accidents with these patent escapes to take any chances. Now there's another inventor who will have to make quite a few changes in his apparatus."

The man who had patented the fire escape had been in a frenzy of fear when he saw Paul slipping, and, now that he knew the young actor was safe, he began to explain how something unforeseen had occurred, and that it would never happen again.

"Did you get that, Russ?" the manager wanted to know, for he thought the operator, in his anxiety over Paul, might have forgotten to turn the handle of the machine.

"Every move," was the reassuring answer. "It will make a dandy film. But I'm mighty glad it turned out as it did."

"So am I," said the manager. "I guess that will be about all for Paul to-day. His nerves must be on edge."

Paul declared that they were not, however, and wanted to go on with the rest of the film, which included the showing of other, but less dangerous, inventions.

"No, you take the rest of the day off," directed the manager.

Laura Lee Hope

"There is no great rush about this."

The crowd pressed curiously about Paul and the others of the moving picture company, and, as Ruth and Alice were getting hemmed in, Mr. Pertell called a taxicab and sent them home in it.

"Report at the studio to-morrow," he called.

"Did you have any more trouble with that spy?" asked Alice, as the vehicle moved away.

"No," he answered. "I guess they'll quit, now that they know I have found them out."

The next day Paul finished with his invention-film, being required to do a number of "funny stunts," such as shaving with a new safety razor that did anything but what it was intended for; trying a new wardrobe trunk, that unexpectedly closed up with him inside of it, and such things as that. Some of the inventions were real, and others were "faked" for the occasion, to make a "comic" film.

But nothing as risky as the rope escape was tried, though probably had Paul been required to go through an equally hazardous feat he would not have balked. Moving picture actors often take very big chances, and the public, looking at the finished film, little realize it.

"I have something for you to-day I think you'll like," said Mr. Pertell to Ruth and Alice, as they reported at the studio.

"I hope it is outdoor stuff," ventured Alice. "It is just glorious to-day!"

Moving picture work is referred to as "stuff." Thus scenes at a river or lake are "water stuff," and if a play should take place in a desert the action would be termed "desert stuff," and so on.

"Well, I'm sorry, but only part of it, and a very little at that, is outdoor stuff," replied Mr. Pertell. "The action of this play takes place in a shirt waist factory. And I've got the use of a real factory where you two girls will pose and go through the 'business.' You're to be shirt waist operators, and I'll explain the story to you later."

"I can't sew very well," confessed Alice, "and I never made but one shirt waist in my life—I couldn't wear it after it was done," she added.

"You don't really have to sew," explained Mr. Pertell. "It is all machine work, anyhow. You and Ruth will sit at the machines in the factory with the other girls. Miss Pennington and Miss Dixon are also to be operators, but you two are the main characters. The machines work by a small electric motor, and all you have to do is to push some cloth along under the needle. You can do that."

"I guess so," agreed Alice.

"The forewoman will rehearse you a bit," Mr. Pertell went on. "The scene at the machines only takes a few moments— just a little strip of film. Then the scene changes to another part of the factory. I think it will make a good film. The story is called 'The Eye of a Needle.' It's really quite clever and by a new writer. I think it will make a hit."

Ruth and Alice, as well as the others, were told more in detail what action the play required, and the next day they were ready for their parts. They went to the factory accompanied by the two former vaudeville actresses, and by

Russ and Paul. The latter was to take the part of one of the male employees of the concern.

Ruth and Alice found themselves in a room filled with sewing machines, at which sat girls and women busily engaged in stitching on shirt waists. There was the hum of the small electric motors that operated the machines, and the click and hum of the machines themselves.

A murmur ran around the room on the entrance of the players, but the operators had been told what to expect and what to do. They were to be in the pictures, too.

Ruth and Alice, with Miss Pennington and Miss Dixon, were given machines close to the camera, as they were the principal characters, and interest centered in them.

"Just guide the cloth through under the needle," the fore-woman explained, as she started the motors on the girls' machines.

"Ready!" called Mr. Pertell to Russ, who stood beside the camera. The action of the play began, as Russ clicked away at the handle of his machine.

Suddenly a girl screamed.

"Oh, what is it?" demanded Miss Pennington, jumping up.

"Sit down! You'll spoil the film!" cried Mr. Pertell.

There was a little confusion for a moment.

"It's only one of the girls who has run a needle into her finger," the forewoman explained. "It often happens. We take care of them right here."

"All right—get that in, Russ," suggested Mr. Pertell. "It will make it seem much more natural."

The girl's injury was a slight one, and Russ got on the film the action of her being attended in the room set aside for the treatment of injured employes.

"I'll have something written in the script to fit to that," said Mr. Pertell, as the action of the play resumed.

The plot of the little drama called upon Miss Pennington to write a note to Alice, pretending that it came from a young man, whose name the former vaudeville performer was supposed to forge. Alice was to "register" certain emotions, and to show the note to Ruth. Then Miss Dixon came into the scene, the sewing machines were deserted and, for a moment, there was an excited conference.

Considerable dramatic action was called for, and this was well done by the girls, while the real operatives looked on in simulated surprise as they kept at their work.

The play was almost over, when from a far corner of the room came a startled cry.

"Someone else hurt with a needle, I wonder?" queried Paul, as he stood near Alice's machine.

"I hope not," she answered.

And then the whole room was thrown into panic as the cry broke out:

"Fire! Fire! The building is on fire!"

Shrill screams drowned out the rest of the alarm, but as Ruth,

Alice and the others of the moving picture company looked around they saw a cloud of smoke at the rear of the big room.

CHAPTER V

A MIX-UP

"Stand still! Don't rush! Form in line!"

Sharp and crisp came the words of the forewoman. The screaming of the girls ceased almost instantly.

Clang! sounded a big gong through the room. Clang! Clang!

"Fire drill!" called the efficient forewoman, and afterward Ruth and Alice felt what a blessing it was she kept her wits about her. "Fire drill! Form in line and march to the fire escapes!"

"Oh! Oh, I know I'm going to faint!" cried Miss Pennington. "This is a regular fire trap! All shirt waist factories are. I am going to faint!"

"Miss Dixon, just—slap her!" called Alice.

"Oh, Alice!" remonstrated Ruth, looking about with frightened eyes.

"It's the only way to bring her to her senses!" retorted the younger girl. And to the eternal credit of Miss Dixon be it said that she did slap her friend Miss Pennington, and she slapped her with sufficient energy to prevent the fainting fit, even as a sip of aromatic spirits of ammonia might have done.

"Fire drill! Form lines! March!" again called the forewoman, with the coolness a veteran fireman might have envied.

"Can't we get our wraps?" asked one of the workers.

"No! You can come back for them," was the answer.

"But it—it's a real fire!" someone cried. "Our things will be burned up!"

"It isn't a fire at all—it's only a drill!" insisted the forewoman. "And, even if it were real, and your things were burned, the company would replace them for you.

"To the fire escapes! March!"

In spite of the forewoman's assertion that it was only a fire drill the pall of smoke in the corner of the room spread apace, and there was the smell of fire, as well as the crackle of flames.

"This way, girls," called Mr. Pertell to his four actresses. "Here's a fire escape over here."

"Excuse me," said the forewoman, firmly. "But please have your company follow my girls. They know just which way to go, and if your actresses make any change it may result in confusion, and—"

"I understand," responded Mr. Pertell, at once. "Girls, consider yourselves shirt waist operatives, and do as the others do," he concluded. He stood aside, as a sailor might on a sinking ship, when the order "women and children first" is given. Paul took his place at the manager's side, waving his hand reassuringly to Ruth and Alice.

"Oh—Oh, must we go with them? Can't we go to that fire escape?" faltered Miss Pennington, who seemed to have entirely recovered from her desire to faint.

"That is for the operatives on the upper floor," explained the forewoman. "If you will follow my girls you will be all right. There are plenty of fire escapes for all."

"Come on!" called Alice, as she marched behind the nearest shirt waist girls. "There is no danger—and plenty of time."

"That's the way to talk!" declared the forewoman, admiringly.

But, even as she spoke, there was a burst of flame through the cloud of smoke. Several girls screamed and those nearest the fire hung back.

"Steady! Go on! There is no danger!" the forewoman called.

"Are you getting this, Russ?" asked Mr. Pertell of the young camera expert.

"Every move!" was the enthusiastic answer. "It's too good a chance to miss, and I guess there is really no danger."

He continued to grind away at the camera while the girls, now in orderly array, marched to the fire escapes and so down and out of the building. Ruth, Alice and the two other actresses went with them. And not until the last girl had left the room did the forewoman make a move toward

Laura Lee Hope

the escape.

"You gentlemen will please leave now," she said.

"After you," returned Mr. Pertell, with a look of admiration in his eyes.

"No," she said, firmly. "The rules of the fire drill require that I leave the room last. You will please go first."

"But, my dear young lady!" exclaimed the manager, "this is not a drill—it is a real fire!"

"I know it," she said, quietly. "But that makes no difference. I must leave last. You will kindly go ahead."

"I guess we'll have to, Russ," remarked the manager. "But I don't like it."

"Those are the rules," insisted the forewoman, and she would not go out on the fire escape until Russ, Paul and Mr. Pertell had preceded her.

By this time the street below was filled with fire apparatus, puffing, clanging and whistling. And not until the girls were down and out of the building did they realize what a big fire it was. For the entire structure was now ablaze.

Fortunately the same efficient fire drill instituted by the forewoman on the floor where Ruth and Alice had been prevailed in other parts of the building, and not a life was lost, though there were many narrow escapes.

And you may well believe that Russ did not miss this opportunity to get moving pictures. Of course the plot of the play had been spoiled by the fire, but a far better drama than the one originally planned was afterward made of it.

As the building continued to burn Russ found that he was not going to have film enough. He sent Paul for a new supply and also to telephone for another operator from the Comet studio, so that pictures of the big fire from various viewpoints might be secured.

And it was a big fire—one of the largest in New York in many years, but aside from a few persons who received minor injuries there was none seriously hurt. The Comet concern scored heavily in making films of the blaze.

"Well, that was one exciting day, yesterday," remarked Russ the next morning at the studio. "I never worked so hard, not even when we were lost in Florida."

"I had a premonition something would happen," declared Mr. Sneed, as he was making up for his part in a play. "When I got up yesterday morning I stepped on my collar button, and that's always a sure sign something will happen."

"It's sometimes a sign you'll be late for rehearsal if you don't find the collar button," laughed Paul.

Orders for the day's work were issued, and Paul, Ruth, Alice and Mr. Bunn found that they had to go to the Grand Central Terminal where, once before, some film pictures had been made.

"There is quite a complicated plot to this play," explained Mr. Pertell, in issuing his instructions. "Mr. Bunn has some valuable papers, and Paul, as the villain, takes them from his pocket in the station. That starts the action."

Fully instructed what to do, the moving picture girls, with

Paul and Russ, went up to Forty-second street.

As the use of the train platforms was not required in this act of the play nothing was said to the station authorities, but Mr. Bunn, with Alice and Ruth, mingled with the crowds, as though they were ordinary travelers.

The operator began taking the necessary pictures, and then came Paul's "cue" to abstract the papers.

He had done it successfully from Mr. Bunn's pocket, seemingly without the knowledge of the actor, and Paul was going on with the rest of the "business," when a policeman stepped up and clapping his hand on Paul's shoulder exclaimed:

"I want you, young man! I saw you take those papers. You're under arrest!"

"But—but it's for the movies!" cried Paul, not wishing the scene spoiled.

"Tell that to the taxicab man! I've heard that yarn before! You come with me. And you too," he added to Mr. Bunn. "I want you for a witness. You've been robbed!"

CHAPTER VI

THE AUTO SMASH

"The scene will be spoiled!" exclaimed Alice, as she saw a crowd surge up when the officer grasped Paul.

"Too bad!" declared Ruth.

"Keep away—get back, please!" cried Russ, as he saw his camera screened by the throng.

"You come along with me!" the officer kept insisting to Paul, dragging him along toward the doors of the station. "Hi, Jim!" he called to a man in plain clothes, evidently a detective. "Grab the other fellow; will you? I've got the pickpocket!" and he nodded to Mr. Bunn, who could not seem to understand that from a simulated robbery it had turned out to be a "real" one.

"I tell you we're moving picture actors!" Paul cried. "There has been no theft!"

"And you expect me to believe that!" sneered the policeman. "You can't get away with that story."

"Well, there's the man who is taking the pictures!" Paul went on, pointing to Russ, who, with a look of chagrin on his face, stood idle beside the camera. He did not want to take a film with this scene in it, for the whole plot of the story would have to be changed to make the policeman fit in.

"Yes, I see him," agreed the officer, nodding at Russ, "and I guess he's in the game with you. I'll take him into custody, too."

"Yes, and you'll get yourself into a whole lot of trouble!" said Paul, vigorously. "You're making a mistake!"

"I'll take that chance," observed the officer, with evident disbelief.

"What's it all about?" asked the detective, sauntering up, while Alice and Ruth, rather alarmed at the turn of affairs, shrank back out of sight behind the crowd, that was increasing every second.

"Pickpocket!" spoke the policeman, laconically. "I saw him rob that elderly gentleman," and he pointed to Mr. Bunn. "And then this fellow has the nerve to say he was only doing a moving picture stunt."

"That's right, and he could see for himself, if he'd take the trouble to look," retorted the young actor. "There's our camera man over there," and he nodded toward Russ. The detective glanced in the same direction, and then a smile came over his somewhat shrewd face, as Russ nodded to him.

"Hello, Dalwood!" exclaimed the detective. Then to the officer—"I guess he's right, Kelly, and you're wrong. I know that young fellow at the camera. He's been at headquarters once or twice helping our rogues' gallery men when their cameras needed fixing."

"Is—is that so?" faltered the officer, and his hold on Paul relaxed.

"That's right," the detective went on. "I guess you've sort of mixed things up, Kelly."

"That's what he has," said Russ. "But if he'll let things go on, and keep this crowd back, I think we can still make the film."

"Oh, I'll do that!" the policeman replied hastily, willing to make amends for the trouble he had caused. "Then it wasn't a case of pocket picking at all?"

"No, we're making a moving picture film," Paul explained. "I took these papers—they're worthless, as you can see," and he showed that the bundle he had extracted from Mr. Bunn's pocket consisted only of some circulars, and blank pieces of paper with imposing looking seals on. But on the film they would appear to be valuable documents.

"Huh! That's a new one on me!" the officer exclaimed. "Now, you people move back!" he cried, "and give 'em a chance to take their pictures. Move back there!"

Affairs had turned in the direction of our friends, and a little later Russ was able to complete the film, from the point where the policeman had stepped in and spoiled it. The small portion that was of no use, however, could be cut out when the film was developed, and the audiences would never be the wiser.

Again Paul went on with his acting from the point where he had been interrupted, and Ruth, Alice and Mr. Bunn did their share. Eventually the film was made.

Laura Lee Hope

"Something new every day!" laughed Paul, as they were coming away from the terminal. "I wonder what will happen next?"

"As long as you don't have to go up in an airship you'll be all right," observed Alice, trying to keep a refractory wisp of hair from coming down into her eyes.

"That's right," agreed Paul, "and yet I wouldn't be surprised to get orders to go up to the clouds any day. In fact, I'm pretty sure we've got to take a queer auto trip soon."

"Is that so? When? Where?" demanded Ruth, pausing a moment to look at a shop window where some lingerie was temptingly displayed.

"I don't know the particulars. I happened to overhear Mr. Pertell talking to Pop Snooks about it. I expect it will be given out in a few days, before Russ has to film it."

The next few days were filled with work for the moving picture actors and actresses. There was much to be done before the Western trip was undertaken, and many of the films made had a bearing on the new play "East and West."

"My idea," announced Mr. Pertell, in explaining some matters to his company, "is to portray briefly the story of the East and West, and to show how the civilization of the East made its way West. I want to show the various sports and industries of both sections, as well as various phases of life and science. Automobiling will be one and—"

"Don't say airships!" interrupted Mr. Sneed.

"That's just what I was going to say," finished Mr. Pertell, with a smile. "I will want some of you to take a trip in an airship. But that will come later."

"I'll never go up!" declared the "grouch."

"Well, we'll settle that later," the manager went on. "Just at present I am going to have some automobile pictures made, and in one of them an auto containing you young ladies," he looked at Ruth and Alice, "goes to smash down a steep hill and over a cliff."

"Oh!" cried Ruth, clutching at her heart.

"How exciting!" exclaimed Alice, apparently not in the least disturbed.

"Yes," said Mr. Pertell, with a smile. "But don't worry. This will be a 'substitute' film. That is, you'll be in the auto up to a certain point. The chauffeur loses control of it, and it starts to run away down hill. Then it is stopped, the camera is closed for a moment until we substitute an old auto for the real one in which you are. There are dummy figures in the old auto, and they are the ones that go to smash over the cliff. Think you can work that, Russ?"

"Oh, yes, I've done those trick pictures before. Where are you going to plant the smash?"

"Oh, over in Jersey. There are several places in the Orange Mountains that will answer. Near Eagle Rock is a good place."

"All right," agreed the young operator. "I'll be ready whenever you are. But where are you going to get the auto that goes to smash, Mr. Pertell?"

"Oh, I bought a second-hand one cheap. It's now being

painted and fixed up to look as much like the good one as possible."

A few days later all was in readiness for taking the auto smash film. The story to be depicted was part of the big "East and West" drama. Ruth and Alice were supposed to be pursued by persons in another auto, and in the smash both girls were to be "injured."

The two automobiles were on hand at the appointed time on a steep slope of the Orange Mountains, where the road turned suddenly near a steep cliff. It was over this cliff that the "smash" would occur.

The auto that would really come to grief was an old rattletrap of a machine, but it would serve the purpose well enough for the film, since only a momentary glimpse of it, and that showing it going at full speed, would be given. The dummy figures, made up to look like Ruth and Alice, were in readiness.

"Now, girls, take your places, if you please," said Mr. Pertell, waving Ruth and Alice toward their car.

"Oh, I'm so nervous!" exclaimed Ruth.

"What about?" asked her sister, as she buttoned her jacket, for the wind was sharp on the hillside.

"Oh, suppose our car doesn't stop in time? Suppose we go over the cliff, instead of the stuffed figures?"

"Don't suppose anything of the kind!" cried Alice, gaily. "Come on—they're waiting for us."

CHAPTER VII

OFF FOR THE WEST

Ruth and Alice, taking their places in what might be termed the "regular" auto, were told just what to do. They were supposed to be escaping from their pursuers, who were in another auto that was to come up from the rear.

Then their chauffeur, in an endeavor to make speed, would go too fast, would not be able to make the turn in the road, and would go over the cliff. But, at the proper time, the dummies and the old auto would be substituted.

"All ready now?" asked Mr. Pertell, when he had carefully repeated his instructions to the girls.

"All ready," answered Alice, and Ruth nodded, though a bit doubtfully. She was really nervous, although she tried not to show it too plainly.

"All ready here," answered Russ, who was beside the camera.

"Then go!" cried the manager, and the auto started.

In order to give the idea of a long chase Russ had to set up his camera in several different places. He changed from one stretch of road to another, the auto being brought to a stop, to wait until he was ready, and then started up again.

But the public saw none of this when the film was exhibited, for only motion was shown, the various sections of the celluloid being joined together in such a way as to preserve the continuity.

"Now ready for the big scene," called Mr. Pertell, after one of these stops. "It's going very well."

Ruth and Alice who, with Paul, were in the regular auto, had shown or "registered" all sorts of emotions during the chase. Sometimes the pursuing auto would be almost up to the one in front, and again it would lag far behind, in order to conform to the requirements of the script, or the story of the film play.

"You will run your car up to here," said Mr. Pertell to the chauffeur of the machine containing Ruth, Alice and Paul. "Then you will stop, and the substitution will be made. Come on with as much speed as is safe, right to this mark," and he indicated a stone in the highway.

"And be sure you *do* stop!" exclaimed Paul, with a short laugh. "That's rather too near the edge of the cliff to suit me."

"I know it is," agreed Mr. Pertell, "It has to be. I only want a few feet of the film showing the actual smash. If it runs too long the public may see the dummies too plainly. I want this as real an accident as it's possible to have it."

"It seems like tempting Providence," murmured Ruth.

"Don't get 'Sneedified'," was the retort of Alice.

Russ had set up his camera to get views of the auto coming down the steep slope, and now, at his signal that all was in readiness, the chauffeur of the car started it again.

"Business! Business!" called Mr. Pertell to the moving picture girls and Paul, meaning that they were to use the proper gestures, and register the desired emotions to coincide with the play.

On rushed the auto, straight toward the dangerous turn in the road. Paul, who had risen to his feet, was talking vigorously to Ruth and Alice, as called for in the scenario. Now and then he would look back, as though to see if the other car was coming.

Suddenly, as the auto was dashing down hill, there came a snap as if some metal part had broken, and the car's speed was quickly increased.

"What is it? Oh, what has happened?" cried Ruth, springing to her feet. But she was at once tossed back on the seat, owing to the swaying of the car, which was going very fast.

"Something's broken!" cried Paul.

"Yes, the foot brake. But I have the emergency one still!" the chauffeur yelled.

"Is there any danger? Shall we jump?" demanded Alice.

"No! Sit still!" the chauffeur cried. "I'll stop her in time, I think."

It was evident the car was beyond control. There was no need of pretending this.

"Look out!" warned Russ, who in his excitement did not forget to work the camera.

"Stop! Stop!" yelled Mr. Pertell. "You're going too far—you'll go over the cliff!"

The chauffeur realized this as well as any one, and he was pulling with all his strength on the emergency brake lever.

"I've got to stop her!" he panted through his clenched teeth. "I've got to stop her!"

Ruth and Alice were in a frenzy of fear now, and Paul, standing up in the swaying auto, and holding to the back of the front seat, was trying desperately to think of some plan whereby he could save the girls.

The car was now at the turn. Now it was beyond the marking stone specified by Mr. Pertell.

"They'll go over the cliff!" shouted Mr. Sneed, who was to take part in the play later.

Mr. Pertell rushed forward as though he would halt the auto by getting in front and pushing it back, and for one wild moment it looked as though there would be a veritable tragedy. But with a last desperate pull on the brake lever, while the metal bands shrilly protested against such strenuous work, the car came to a slow stop.

And so near was it to the fence railing off the descent over the cliff—which fence was, later, to be crashed into by the make-believe auto—so near was the girls' car to this fence that the front wheels bent one of the rails.

"A close call!" said Russ, and his voice was unsteady as he

stepped away from the camera.

Ruth and Alice were pale, and Paul, too, had lost some of his color. But it was Alice who first relieved the strain of the situation.

"A miss is as good as a mile," she said, and tried to laugh, but it was not easy.

"There must be some defect in that brake connection," the chauffeur said, as he got out to look at it.

"Well, as long as we're all right, the film will be so much the better," observed Paul, as he alighted from the car. "It will look realistic enough; won't it, Russ?"

"Indeed it will. I thought sure you were goners; but I kept on grinding away. It will be realistic enough for even Mr. Pertell, I think," and he glanced at the manager.

"I'm awfully sorry this occurred," declared the latter. "I assure you ladies that I never would willingly have let you run such a risk."

"Oh, we know that," responded Ruth, quickly. "It was no one's fault. Only I'm glad daddy wasn't here to see us," she added in a low voice to her sister.

"So am I!" was the reply.

"Now then, you had better get back to New York," went on Mr. Pertell. "This ends the scenes in Jersey, and your nerves must be pretty well shattered," he said, looking at the two girls.

"Oh, I want to stay and watch the other auto go to smash,"

Alice cried. "That will be something worth seeing, especially as no one will be hurt, except the dummies."

"I'll stay, too," said Ruth. "It will be novel to see ourselves as stuffed figures."

Preparations were now made for having the second auto plunge over the cliff. This car was set in the exact position the other had occupied when brought to a stop. The dummy figures were put in, veils effectually concealing the faces. Then the motor was started.

Meanwhile Russ had taken his camera to the foot of the cliff where he could get a view of the car plunging over, and smashing.

"All ready!" came the signal. By means of long wires, which would not show in the finished picture, the gears were thrown in, and the brakes released.

"There she goes!" cried Russ.

The car containing the dummies started off at a fast rate. It crashed through the fence, just as the other car might have done, and the next instant was hurtling through the air.

It turned partly over, one of the dummy figures—that of Ruth—toppled out—and a moment later, with a crash that could be heard a long distance, the auto was crumpled into a shapeless mass at the foot of the cliff.

Russ got every detail of this, and when the wrecked auto caught fire from the burst gasoline tank it added to the effectiveness of the scene, though that feature had not been counted on.

Then several men came rushing up. They had been stationed in readiness for just that purpose, and they picked up the figures of the dummies.

That ended the scene, for the next act took place in a hospital, whither Ruth, Alice and Paul were supposed to be carried. That would be a studio scene, and filmed later.

"Well, that's over," said Mr. Pertell, with a sigh of relief, as he and his company of players prepared to return to New York. A throng of curious bystanders, attracted by the actors and actresses, gathered about the burning auto at the foot of the cliff. As it was of no further service it was left there.

"Well, ladies and gentlemen," announced Mr. Pertell to his assembled company a few days after the auto film had been made, "I am ready now to tell you something of my plans for the Western trip. Arrangements have been about completed, and we leave in a few days."

"Where are we going?" asked Mr. DeVere.

"Our first destination will be a place called Rocky Ranch," the manager went on. "It is a typical Western place, with some broad prairie stretches, and yet near enough to the mountains for diversified scenes. There will be cowboy and Indian pictures to be made, and—"

"*Wild* Indians?" Mr. Sneed wanted to know.

"Not wild enough to scalp you," returned the manager.

"And can I have a gun?" little Tommy cried.

"Indeed and you won't!" said his grandmother, quickly.

"Well, you can be cowboy and have a lasso," promised the manager.

"Oh, goodie!" Tommy exclaimed, dancing about in delight.

"In this play," went on Mr. Pertell, "I want to get scenes showing our progress West, so we will be rather longer on the trip than otherwise. We will wait over on some trains, to make views in particularly good spots. So you may get ready for the journey. Our Eastern scenes are all made, and I want to thank and congratulate you all on their success. It was the good acting of all of you that made the films what they are."

Preparations for the big trip went on apace. Properties and baggage were gotten in readiness, and Ruth and Alice spent days going over their clothes, to decide what to take and what to leave behind.

"Though if I'm to be a cowgirl, and ride ponies, I don't suppose I'll want this," said Alice, holding up a filmy white dress.

"Better take it," advised Ruth, who was seated tailor-fashion before a trunk, which she was packing.

"It crushes too easily," objected the other.

"Fold it around some heavier things," suggested Ruth, "and don't put it in the trunk until the last thing. Oh, I believe I've put my suede slippers in the bottom, and I'll want them to-night. Well, I'll have to dig 'em out, I guess," she sighed.

"No, there they are!" cried Alice, fishing them out from under a pile of stockings. "What have you in them?" she asked her sister, as she saw the slippers were filled with something.

"I always stuff the toes with old stockings," said Ruth. "It keeps them out almost as well as if I used shoe-trees."

"Good idea," laughed her sister.

The packing was over, the trunks were at the station and also was gathered there the moving picture company.

"Ho, for the West!" cried Russ, who was standing with Paul, Ruth and Alice.

"All aboard!" called Mr. Pertell. And, as they moved off toward the train Russ, turning, saw a man staring after the players.

"Look!" said the young operator, in a low voice to Mr. Pertell, "that International Film Company spy—Wilson—is keeping tabs on us!"

Laura Lee Hope

CHAPTER VIII

THE OIL WELL

Mr. Pertell paused and looked back. There on the depot platform stood the man he had caught in his testing room taking notes of the films of the big drama.

"Those fellows mean business!" the manager commented. "They are trying to get my best ideas, I think. It's a wonder they wouldn't originate something themselves!"

"I'd like to have it out with him," declared Russ.

"It would only make trouble," responded the manager. "I think I can stop them in another way. I'll try legal means first, and if they don't work—well, perhaps we can put up some kind of a game on them."

"Let me have a hand in it," begged the young operator. "I want to pay my respects to that fellow."

Wilson, for so it was, had by this time seen that he was observed, and he slunk out of sight behind a pillar. Then, as Mr. Pertell and Russ went to take their places in the coach with the others, a truck, piled with the baggage of the company, came along.

The spy darted out from behind the pillar and with a quick glance noted the destination as shown on the checks.

"So that was his game!" cried Russ. "I'll put a stop to that, all right!"

"It's too late. He's seen, and, anyhow, he could have found out," called Mr. Pertell. But Russ did not stay to hear, for he had made a rush toward the fellow.

He was too late, however, and perhaps it was just as well, as Russ was a bit hot-headed, and there might have been a scene. Wilson, seeing Russ coming, hastily thrust into his pocket a card on which he had evidently been copying the name of the place to which the trunks had been checked, and ran away.

"Come back, Russ," called Mr. Pertell. "You'll miss the train!" for the warning whistle had sounded.

"I wish I had caught him," panted the young operator as he returned. "I never saw a fellow with such nerve."

"His company is in bad shape," said Mr. Pertell. "They have been losing money, and their films are not taking well. They have not much of a company of players, and I suppose they think they can use some of our ideas, and maybe some of our actors and actresses."

"How do you mean—by hiring them away from you?" asked Russ.

"Well, they might do that, though I don't believe the International people will pay the salaries my people are getting. So I think none of them would leave. Even if more money were offered I think my friends would stand by me.

But what I meant was that we'll have to be on the watch to see that they don't actually take some of our films."

"You mean after I have made the reels?"

"No, they might even try, on the sly, to film the action of our players when we're going through some scene."

"Whew!" whistled Russ. "If they do that you could have them arrested."

"Well, be on the watch—that's all."

None of the other members of the company had seen the spy, and Russ and the manager said nothing about him. The train pulled out of the station, and thus the Western trip was begun.

Mr. Pertell planned to stop off with his company at several places and make films along the way. This was in accord with his idea of showing a big drama indicating the development of this country from East to West. The rush of the gold seekers, and the advance of the farmers to take up Government claims, were to be depicted, along with many other scenes.

One stop was made in the coal mining regions of Pennsylvania, near Scranton, and there some fine films were obtained. In one scene Ruth and Alice were shown in the interior of a mine, with the black coal all about them. Powerful electric lights gave the necessary illumination.

"I'd like to get a scene showing an explosion," said Russ, as they left the coal regions.

"Why, Russ Dalwood!" cried Ruth. "I'm surprised at you!"

"Oh, I don't mean by accident," he replied, quickly. "In fact, a little one would do. And I don't want one to happen on my account. But if there's going to be an accident I wish I could be on hand to film it."

"Oh, that's different," said Ruth, with a smile. "But I'm glad there is no accident."

Three days had been spent in and around Scranton, and now the moving picture players were ready to start off again. Mr. Pertell was reconsidering some plans he and Russ had talked over, and it had not been definitely decided what to do as yet.

"We'll just keep on," said the manager, "and perhaps something will turn up to give me an idea for a novel film."

They had taken a train on a small branch line of the railroad to connect with a through express, and about an hour after starting, and when about half-way to the junction, they came to a sudden stop.

"Ha! An accident!" cried Russ, reaching for the small camera he kept for emergencies.

"Wait, I'll come with you," said the manager. "We may be able to make it into a film."

But when they got on the outside, followed by several of the members of the company, they saw no signs of anything wrong. There was no other train in sight, so there could have been no collision, and their own train was safely on the track. Off to one side, however, gathered about a tall structure of wood, was a knot of people.

"What's the matter?" asked Russ of one of the trainmen.

"They're going to shoot an oil well over there," was the answer, "and it's so close to the track that they signalled us to stop."

"Why didn't they wait until we got past?" asked Mr. DeVere who, with his daughters, had gone out to see what caused the delay.

"Why, they had already lowered the charge of nitro-glycerine into the well," the brakeman explained, "and something has gone wrong. The shot didn't go off, and they're afraid it may at any minute. So they're holding us back a little while."

"Is that an oil well?" asked Alice, pointing to the tall, wooden structure.

"That's the derrick, by which the drill is worked—yes, Miss," the brakeman said. "They bore down through the sand and rock until they think they're close to the oil. Then they blow out what rock and earth remains, with nitro-glycerine. The well may be a 'spouter,' or they may have to pump. Can't tell until after they fire the shot. I guess she's going off!" he added quickly. "Look at 'em run!"

"I've got my idea!" exclaimed Mr. Pertell. "We'll have a film of boring for oil. That will fit in well with my big drama. Get the company together, Pop," he said to the property man. "And, Russ, get ready to film the shooting of the oil well."

CHAPTER IX

THE RIVALS

Though there was a rush of spectators away from the oil well it appeared to be a false alarm, for nothing happened, and Mr. Pertell, who was afraid the well would "spout" before he could get his company of players on the scene, was relieved when he heard one of the workmen call:

"False alarm. She isn't going off yet."

"Now hurry and get around the well," urged the manager. "I want some of you grouped near it when the oil spouts up."

"Won't it be dangerous?" asked Mr. Sneed. "I don't want to be blown up by nitro-glycerine."

"You needn't get too close," returned Mr. Pertell. "I just want the spouting well as a background."

"It will be all right if you keep about thirty feet back," said one of the well borers.

"How do you shoot a well?" asked Paul, while Russ was getting ready his camera.

"By using nitro-glycerine," was the answer. "This explosive comes in tin cans, about ten feet long and about five inches in diameter. We lower these cannisters down into the iron pipe that extends to the bottom of the well."

"How deep?" queried Alice.

"Oh, a well may run anywhere from three hundred to three thousand feet, or even more. This one is about one thousand. We have about a hundred quarts of nitro-glycerine down in the pipes now; but it hasn't gone off yet."

"Can you—er—tell me when it *will* go off?" asked Mr. Sneed, looking about him nervously.

"Any minute, if not sooner," replied the oil man, with a smile. "Oh, don't run—you're safe here," he added, as Mr. Sneed began to move away. At the same time Claude Towne, the "swell" of the company, exclaimed:

"I'm not going to stay here and get this new suit spoiled by the oil." He was very careful of his attire.

"Oh, the oil won't spray as far as this," the workman assured him.

"How do they explode the glycerine?" asked Mr. DeVere.

"Well, the old plan used to be to drop an iron weight called a 'go-devil,' down on top of the cannisters containing the explosive. The top can was fitted with a firing head, and when the iron weight hit this, after a long fall, it would explode, and the concussion would set off the rest of the glycerine."

"But this time we tried a new plan. We used a 'go-devil-squib.' That's a sort of torpedo, holding about a quart of the glycerine, and it has a firing head of its own. We drop that down the pipe and when it hits on the top cannister it goes off, and sets off the rest of the explosive. But, somehow, it didn't work this time. The charge missed fire, so now we're going to drop down an old fashioned 'go-devil' and see what happens."

Mr. Pertell asked, and readily obtained, permission to make moving pictures of the shooting of the well, and was also accorded the privilege of posing his company at the scene when the well did "spout."

"I'll have to think up some sort of a scenario to go with it," the manager said.

"Have some poor man get rich suddenly by striking oil on his land," suggested Russ, "and then show what he does with his money. You can easily get the later scenes."

"Good idea—I will," exclaimed the manager. "We'll use this as the first, or opening, scene in—let me see, we'll call it 'The Rise and Fall of the Kerosene King.' How's that?"

"Good!" cried Mr. DeVere.

"All right. Paul, you'll be the king. But you'll have to start as a poor lad, and those good clothes won't do. Slip on a pair of greasy overalls—borrow them from one of the men—then you'll look more natural."

Paul was soon fitted out as one of the oil men, and then, after a brief rehearsal, the improvised drama was ready to be taken on the sensitive film. A few preliminary scenes were made by Russ, and then, as word was given that the iron weight was about to be dropped on the cans of glycerine in the well-pipes, Mr. Pertell got his company as close to the derrick as

Laura Lee Hope

was safe. Then, while Russ clicked away at the camera, one of the workmen called:

"Let her go!"

A man dropped the iron weight down the pipe and ran.

"Look out, everybody!" he cried as he sprang away.

"Are we safe here?" Mr. Sneed asked anxiously.

"You're all right," one of the workmen assured him.

"Oh, I'm so nervous!" faltered Ruth.

"No need of it," answered Alice, as she leaned forward to watch the spouting of the oil from the well.

There was a dull rumble beneath the surface of the earth. The ground seemed to heave and shake. It trembled, and Miss Pennington and Miss Dixon looked at each other with frightened eyes.

"It—it's like an earthquake," observed Ruth.

"Oh, look!" cried Alice.

At that moment something like a dark cloud shot upward from the pipes and spread out, plume-fashion. At the same moment the air was filled with the rank odor of oil and gas.

"She's a spouter! She's a spouter!" cried the men, in delight.

"Cap her up!" came the command.

But it was not easy to do at first, so great was the flow of oil, and considerable had run to waste when the internal pressure of natural gas, which forced out the oil, was reduced sufficiently to allow of the pipe being capped, and the flow of petroleum regulated.

All this time Russ had continued to get pictures of the novel scene, and Paul, as the Kerosene King, went through the act that had been improvised for him, the others of the company doing their share.

"This will make a novel film," said Mr. Pertell in satisfied tones. "I hope you got it all, Russ."

"Every bit. I think the views showing the oil spouting up will be first rate."

"But what are you using two cameras for?" asked Mr. DeVere.

"Two cameras?" repeated Mr. Pertell, questioningly.

"Yes, there's a man over there with another machine," and he pointed to a little hill, not far off, where stood a man working away at the handle of a machine similar to the one Russ was using. And this camera was pointed directly at the oil well and at the Comet players.

"What does that mean?" cried Mr. Pertell. "I didn't order two films made, and besides—"

"That isn't one of our men!" interrupted Russ, as he sprang away from his camera.

"Who is it?" Mr. Pertell wanted to know.

"It's one of our rivals. Someone from the International

concern!" cried Russ. "They've followed us to steal some more of our ideas!"

"You're right!" shouted Mr. Pertell. "This will have to stop!"

Together he and Russ, followed by Paul, made a dash in the direction of the rival photographer. But the latter saw them coming, and hastily picking up his machine he ran toward a clump of woods not far off. And by the time his pursuers reached there he was not to be found, though they searched about for some time.

CHAPTER X

THE CYCLONE

"All aboard!" called the conductor of the way train that had been held up to allow the shooting of the oil well. "All board!"

"Come," summoned Mr. Pertell to his moving picture players. "We'll get along now. That stop was a lucky one for us."

The train could now proceed, all danger from the delayed charge in the well being over. Just what had caused it to "hang fire" was never learned. But the shooting of the well was a success, and as the train pulled out, Paul having gotten rid of his borrowed clothes, the workmen were seen hurrying about, taking care of the valuable flow of petroleum.

"What do you make of the action of that International man?" asked Russ, as he took a seat beside the manager.

"I don't know what to make of those fellows," was the answer. "They must be following us pretty closely; but I don't see how they knew we were going to film the oil well."

"They didn't know it," decided Russ. "They've had a spy on

our trail, following us; that's how it was done. You know we saw that fellow Wilson looking at the destination marked on the baggage checks. He probably sent word to the concern and they started out a camera man to follow us. It would have to be someone we hadn't seen before, so of course Wilson himself would not do, though I understand he can operate a machine fairly well."

"I guess you've got the right idea," agreed Mr. Pertell. "This fellow, whoever he was, made inquiries and learned where we were headed for. Then with his camera he simply kept on the same train with us."

"And when we stopped here to get the oil well pictures," resumed Russ, "he trailed along and set up his machine. He got all the benefit of our players' acting and his company wasn't out a cent for salaries or transportation. Of course he probably had as good a right to get pictures of the well as we did."

"But not to film my company!" exclaimed Mr. Pertell, with energy. "I won't stand for that; I'll have a stop put to it!"

"First I'm afraid we'll have to catch him," observed Russ. "He certainly made himself scarce when we ran after him."

"Well, he isn't on this train, that's sure," went on the manager, "and he'll have some trouble picking up our trail after this."

"How's that?" asked Russ.

"Why, I'm going to change our plans. We'll skip the next stop. I was going to go up around the Great Lakes and make part of a drama there, showing the effect the lakes and their trade had on the growth of our country. Now I'll wait until we are on our way back from Rocky Ranch."

"That will be a good idea," agreed the young camera operator. "Those International people must be pretty hard put to it to steal your ideas."

"They are," said Mr. Pertell. "They want to do me an injury. I had some trouble with them years ago, and I won out in a lawsuit. Since then they have been injuring me every chance they could get; but it really amounted to little until lately. Now they are evidently getting desperate, and they are using every means to make trouble for me."

"Well, we'll just have to be on the lookout for them at every turn," Russ declared.

Owing to the decision of Mr. Pertell that he would not, at this time, take his company to the Great Lakes, a change in the route had to be made. This necessitated stopping off for one night at a small country town, where the company put up at the only hotel the place afforded.

"What a miserable place!" exclaimed Miss Pennington, tilting up her head when she entered the office with the others.

"And such a horrid smell!" added Miss Dixon, as she stripped off her long gloves with an air of being used to dining every day at the most exclusive hotels. "I believe they are actually cooking—cabbage, Pearl."

"I agree with you, my dear! Isn't it awful! Can it be—cabbage?"

"Yah! Dot's right!" exclaimed Mr. Switzer, rubbing his hands. "Dot's cabbage, all right—sauerkraut, too. Goot!"

"Ugh!" protested Miss Pennington, making a gesture of annoyance.

"I am glat dot ve come here," went on the German. "I haf not hat any sauerkraut—dot is, not any to mention of—since ve left New York."

"Why, I saw you eating some the other day," laughed Paul, as the odor of cooking cabbage became more pronounced from the hotel kitchen.

"Oh, yes, I hat a leetle—yust enough to know der taste of it," agreed the German, with a genial smile. "But I ain't really hat vot you could call a meal of it."

"You're like a man I heard of," said Russ, joining in the talk. "He was a German farmer, I guess, and when his neighbor asked him if he was putting away any sauerkraut that season the German answered: 'No, ve ain't put none down to speak of dis season. Only yust seven or eight barrels in case of sickness!'"

"Goot! Goot! Dot vos a real German!" laughed Mr. Switzer.

There was sauerkraut for supper that night, and the German actor certainly ate enough to ward off any possible illness. And, in spite of the rather homely character of the hotel, the meal was an excellent one, and the moving picture players were more comfortable in the matter of rooms than they had expected. About the only ones to find fault were Miss Pennington, Miss Dixon, and Mr. Sneed. But they would have had some objection to offer in almost any place, so it did not much matter.

Plans were made for taking a train early next morning, to continue on out West, but something occurred to delay matters, though it resulted in the making of an excellent film.

It was just before everyone was ready for breakfast when Ruth, thinking she heard her sister's knock sharply on the door, opened it.

Instead of confronting Alice, Ruth jumped back in terror as she saw a bear standing upright in the hall opposite her door.

"Oh! Oh!" she screamed as the beast put out his red tongue. "Help! A bear! A bear!" and she slammed her door shut with such energy that she knocked a picture from the wall. Ruth shot home the bolt, and then, in a frenzy of fear, pulled the washstand against the door.

"What is it? Oh, what is it?" cried Alice from her apartment across the corridor. "What is it, Ruth?" for she had heard her sister's frantic appeal, though not catching the words.

"Don't open your door! Don't open you door!" begged Ruth. "There's a bear in the hall!"

"A bear?"

"Yes, a great big one!"

But in spite of this Alice did open her door a little. She closed it quickly enough, however, at the sight of the shaggy brown creature and, pounding on the door of her father's room, which connected with hers, she cried;

"Daddy, get help, quick! There's a bear in the hall!"

There was a speaking tube from the actor's apartment to the hotel office, and he was soon transferring his daughter's message down this.

Meanwhile Mr. Sneed, coming out of his room from the lower end of the hall, encountered the beast, and turned back with a yell. He nearly collided with Mr. Towne, who was at that moment coming out of his room, faultlessly attired, even to a heavy walking stick.

"Look out!" cried Mr. Sneed, racing along.

"What is it?" asked Mr. Towne.

"A bear. Look out! Here he comes!"

And, in fact, the bear was shuffling down the hall, his head lolling from side to side, and his red tongue hanging out.

Either Mr. Towne did not hear what Mr. Sneed said, or he was so surprised that he did not think to run, for he stood there and, a moment later, the big beast confronted him. Stretching out his paw the animal took from the nerveless hands of the actor the heavy walking stick, and, shouldering it, began to march around in a circle.

Then the hotel proprietor, having been alarmed by Mr. DeVere, came up on the run. As soon as he saw the bear marching around he broke into a laugh.

"That's a trained bear!" he exclaimed. "It belongs to that Italian who stopped here last night. I made him chain the brute out in the wagon shed, but I guess he got loose. That bear won't hurt you. I've seen him before. Tony, the Italian who owns him, often stops here with him when he's traveling around giving exhibitions. He's real gentle. Down, Bruno!" commanded the hotel man, and the bear, with a grunt, dropped on all fours.

Alice, hearing this talk, opened her door, and then called to

Ruth that there was no danger. Mr. Sneed was induced to return, and when Tony himself came to get his escaped pet Mr. Towne's cane was returned to him. The bear had taken it for the pole he was used to performing with.

"You want to chain your bear up tighter, Tony," chided the hotel man as the Italian led Bruno away.

"Ah, yes. Bruno, he ees a very bad-a-de bear! I wheep heem for dese."

"Oh, don't!" pleaded Alice. "He didn't mean anything wrong."

"No, mees, but he very bad, just-a de same. He make-a you to be a-skeert."

"Oh, it's all over now," declared Ruth, who ventured out, seeing that the bear was in leash. "But I *was* frightened for a moment."

"I don't blame you," said Paul, as he heard what had happened. "Rather an unusual morning caller, Ruth."

"Say! I've got an idea!" cried Mr. Pertell, who had come out by this time. "We'll have a film with the bear in it. A sort of Little Red Riding Hood story for children. Something simple, but it will be great to have a real bear in it. Tony, will you let us use Bruno?"

"Of a course, Signor. I make up for de scare. Bruno he do-a just-a whatever you tell. He very good-a bear—sometimes!" and he shrugged his shoulders, philosophically.

"Very well, then, we'll wait over another train, and I'll get up some little scenario with a bear in it. Mr. Sneed, you will take the part of the bear's keeper, and Miss Alice—"

"No, sir!" cried Mr. Sneed. "No bears for me. I won't act with one. Why, he'd claw me to pieces!"

"Ah, no, Signor!" interrupted Tony. "Bruno he very gentle just-a like-a de little babe. He no hurt-a you, Signor."

"Well, I'm not going to take any chances," declared the "grouch." "This is too dangerous."

"Ha! I am not afraid!" cried Mr. Switzer. "I vill act mit der bear alretty yet," and to prove that he was not afraid he fed the big animal some pretzels, without which the German actor seldom went abroad.

And, a little later, Russ made a film, in which the bear was one of the central figures. Alice took part in it, and the simple little play made quite a hit when shown.

"You seem to have the happy faculty of making use of everything that comes your way—accidentally or not," remarked Mr. DeVere to Mr. Pertell, when the company was once more under way in the train.

"You have to in the moving picture business," chuckled Mr. Pertell. "That's the secret of success. You never can tell when something will go wrong with a play you have planned carefully and rehearsed well. So you must be ready to take advantage of every change in situation. Also, you must be ready to seize on every opportunity that comes your way."

"You certainly seized on that bear," agreed Mr. DeVere.

"I'm glad he wasn't a wild one," went on the manager. "I am sorry your daughters were frightened—"

"Oh, pray do not mention it," the actor said. "They are getting used to strange experiences in this moving picture work."

"And I want to tell you they are doing most excellently," the manager went on. "I have had many actresses of experience who could not do half as well as Miss Ruth and Miss Alice. I congratulate you!"

Little of moment occurred during the rest of the trip; that is, until the next stopping place was reached. This was at a place in Kansas where Mr. Pertell planned to have some farming operations shown as a background to a certain part in the big drama.

On the way a careful watch had been kept for the appearance of the spies, or camera operators, of the International company, but no trace of them had been seen.

There were no hotels in Fostoria, where the Kansas stop was made, and the company was accommodated at two farm-houses close together. A number of scenes were to be made, with these houses and outbuildings figuring in them.

"Isn't it nice here?" asked Alice as she and Ruth were in their room on the morning after their arrival, getting ready for breakfast.

"It does seem so," agreed the older girl, as she leaned over with her hair hanging in front of her while she combed it out.

"Such wide, open spaces," went on Alice. "Plenty of fresh air here."

"Too much!" laughed Ruth. "Grab that waist of mine; will you, Alice? It's going out of the window on the breeze."

Alice was just in time to prevent the garment from fluttering out of the room, for the breeze was certainly strong.

As the younger girl turned back to hand her sister the waist she exclaimed:

"Oh, what a queer looking cloud! And what a funny yellow light there is, all about. Look, Ruth."

"Isn't it?" agreed Ruth, as she coiled her hair on top of her head. "It looks like a storm."

Off in the west was a bank of yellowish clouds that seemed rolling and tumbling over and over in their eagerness to advance. At the same time there was a sobbing and moaning sound to the wind.

"Oh, Alice. I think there is going to be a terrible storm," gasped Ruth a moment later, suddenly realizingly that danger impended.

Indeed the wind was rising rapidly, and the clouds increased in size. Now confused shouts could be heard out in the farmyard, and some men were running about, rounding up a bunch of cows.

"What's the matter?" called Mr. Pertell, coming out on the side porch.

"Cyclone coming!" answered the proprietor of the farm. "It's going to be a bad one, too!"

CHAPTER XI

AT ROCKY RANCH

With a howl, a rush and a roar the storm was upon them. Never had the moving picture girls or their friends ever seen, heard or imagined such a violent wind.

The sky was overcast with yellowish clouds, edged with black, which were torn and twisted in swirling circles by the gale. The air itself seemed tinged with a sickly green that struck terror to the girls' hearts.

There was a crash that rose high above the howl of the wind, and someone called:

"There goes the roof off the corn crib!"

Inside the house there were confused shouts and calls. The house itself rocked and swayed.

"Oh, what shall we do?" sobbed Ruth.

"Let's go out, before it falls down on us," cried Alice.

Clinging to each other they made their way downstairs. Their father came after them, followed by other members of the moving picture company.

"Is—is there any safe place?" faltered Mr. Sneed, as he look anxiously about.

"The cyclone cellar," answered one of the farm men. "All hands had better take to that. We're out of the path of the worst of the 'twister,' but it's best to take no chances. To the cyclone cellar!"

"Where is it?" asked Mr. Bunn, looking around the room, as though the place of refuge were kept inside the house.

"There!" cried the man, pointing to a small mound of earth, in which was set a sort of trap door. "Go down in there!"

A number of farm hands, as well as members of the family, were making for this haven. It was a veritable cellar, covered over, and used for just such emergencies. A flight of steps led down into it.

"Where are you going, Russ?" cried Ruth, as she saw the young operator turn from the side of the porch where he had been standing.

"For my camera!" he answered, shouting so as to be heard above the noise of the wind. "I'm going to film this—too good a chance to lose."

"But you—you may be hurt!" she faltered.

"I'll take a chance," he replied, as he turned into the house.

Into the cyclone cellar rushed the frightened members of the film company, as well as the farmer's family and helpers.

The wind was howling and shrieking, and several crashes told of further damage being done to the buildings.

Russ, in spite of the commands of Mr. Pertell, set up his camera to get pictures of a cyclone in actual operation. The bending, and in some cases breaking, trees showed the great force of the wind, and the unroofing and demolishing of small outbuildings gave further evidence of the power of the storm.

Russ took his position in an open spot, where he would be in less danger, and got picture after picture, showing the retreat into the underground place of refuge.

The wind was so strong that he had to force the legs of his camera tripod deep into the earth to prevent the apparatus from being blown over.

With a crash the roof of one of the smaller barns was sent sailing far away in the air, and Russ got a fine view of this, though he narrowly escaped being hit by a piece of wood.

"Russ, come in here!" called Mr. Pertell, through a crack in the trap door of the cyclone cellar. "I forbid you to risk your life any further."

"Just a minute!" begged the operator.

"Please come!" cried Ruth.

"All right," he answered, and catching up his camera he took his place in the cellar. And then, as suddenly as it had come up, the wind storm died away. The sullen black and yellow clouds passed onward, and the sun came out. Those in the cellar emerged.

Laura Lee Hope

"Well, it might have been worse," the farmer said, as he looked about. Considerable damage had been done, but his place, and that of his neighbor, were out of the direct path of the cyclone, so the larger buildings escaped. No one was hurt and after the excitement Russ went about, making views of the demolished places, and of the standing grain, which had been blown almost flat.

"I don't believe I'd like to live in Kansas," said Ruth as she re-arranged her hair, tossed about by the wind.

"Nor I," laughed Alice, in a similar plight.

"Oh, we get used to it," remarked the farmer, with a laugh. Yet how he could laugh as he surveyed the ruins of his buildings was rather strange. "We don't get a 'twister' every day," he went on, "and we're glad when we escape alive. A few shacks more or less don't matter. We count on that. I'm sorry you folks got such a bad opinion of Kansas, though."

"Well, we'll give her a chance to redeem herself," said Mr. Pertell. "I guess we'll have to change some of our plans."

"Oh, don't let this storm hinder you," urged the farmer. "We won't have another in a couple of years. Once a cyclone sweeps over a place we feel relieved. It doesn't often pay a return visit."

He and his men were soon busy taking an account of the damage done which, fortunately, was not as great as seemed at first. One cow had been killed, but the farmer remarked, philosophically, that anyhow he was to have sent her to the butcher shortly.

There was a little delay in making the moving pictures, but finally the work of getting out the films was under way, and, if anything, the storm rendered them more effective. Russ was able to work in the views he took of the cyclone, and altogether the drama that was made in Kansas was quite a success.

Once again the players were on their way, and this time they were not to stop until they reached Rocky Ranch, unless something occurred to make it necessary.

The remainder of the trip was uneventful, if we may except a slight accident by which the train was derailed. No one was hurt, however, and it gave Russ a chance to make a little film.

Then, late one afternoon, the party of moving picture players with their properties and baggage reached the station of Altmore, the nearest railroad point to Rocky Ranch. The station was little more than a water tank, and there was not much of a town.

"Oh, what a dreary place!" complained Miss Pennington, as she and her friend Miss Dixon surveyed the scene.

"The end of nowhere," agreed the other. "We shall die of loneliness here."

"I guess it will be lively enough for you out at the ranch," said Mr. Pertell. "But I don't understand why the wagons aren't here to meet us."

"There's something coming down the road," said Russ, pointing to a cloud of dust.

"That's so," agreed the manager.

The dust cloud drew nearer, and then from the center of it

could be heard an excited shouting and yelling, and the galloping of horses. Added to these were the sharp reports of revolvers.

"Something has happened!" cried Mr. Sneed.

"Something *is* happening!" corrected Paul, while Mr. Bunn looked about for a safe retreat.

"Hi! Yi!" were the yells coming from the dust cloud, as the shooting increased. "Hi! Yi!"

"It's an Indian attack!" gasped Miss Pennington. "Oh, where can we hide?"

CHAPTER XII

SUSPICIONS

On came that rushing, swirling, swaying dust-cloud, and out of it continued to come those nerve-racking shouts, yells and shrill screams, accompanied by a fusillade of pistol shots.

"Can anything have occurred to gain us the anger of any of the inhabitants of this place?" asked Mr. DeVere, as he looked about apprehensively, and then at his daughters.

"It sounds like a lot of cowboys," spoke Alice. "At least I've read that's how they act when they paint the town red."

"Oh, Alice!" cried Ruth. "What language!"

"I used it merely in the technical sense," was the retort. "I believe they do not actually use red paint."

"Oh, what shall we do? What shall we do?" cried Miss Pennington.

"I'm going back to New York at once!" sobbed Miss Dixon. "Make that train come back!" she cried to the lone station agent, who, with a set grin on his face, was looking alternately from the group of picture players to the approaching dust cloud that concealed so many weird noises.

But the train was far down the track.

"We must do something!" insisted Mr. Sneed, nervously pacing up and down. "We men must organize and protect the ladies. I think we had better get inside the station and try to hold it against the savages. Pop, you have some guns in the baggage; have you not?"

"Yep!" answered the property man; "but they ain't loaded, and before we could git 'em out those fellers will be here."

"Well, we must protect the ladies at any cost!" insisted Mr. Sneed. "Come with us, we will protect you!" he shouted as he hurried inside the little shed that answered for the station. Probably he wanted to go first to prepare the place for the others. At any rate he was first inside.

"Whoop-ee!"

"Ki-yi!"

"Rah!"

"Bang! Bang! Bang!"

That is the way it sounded. The noise grew louder. The dust-cloud was at the station now. And then, with a fusillade of shots that was well-nigh deafening, the cause of it all came to a sudden stop.

The dust settled and blew away. The cloud parted to reveal several wagons drawn by small but muscular horses. Surrounding the vehicles were half a score of cowboys of the regulation type, save that they did not wear the "chaps," or sheepskin breeches, so often seen in moving picture depictions of the "wild west." Probably the weather was too hot for them, or these cowboys may have gotten rid of them because the garments figured so often in the "movies."

"Cowboys!" cried Russ, with a laugh. "And we thought they were going to attack us!"

"It's one on us, all right," spoke Paul.

"But I have often read of cowboys going on a—on a rampage, I believe it is called—or is it stampede?" asked Miss Dixon, as she stood behind Paul.

"Rampage is right," he informed her.

"Well, maybe that's what they're on now, and they will shoot us after all," she resumed. "Oh, there's one looking right at me!" and she covered her face with her be-ringed hands.

"Probably he hasn't seen a pretty girl in a long time," said Paul, for Miss Dixon was pretty, in a way.

"Oh!" she exclaimed again—and took down her hands.

"And one of them is loading his pistol!" cried Miss Pennington. "Oh, dear!"

"I guess they'll have to load up all around after the shots they fired," laughed Russ. "I wonder what in the world it's all about, anyhow?"

He learned a moment later.

One of the cowboys, evidently the leader, rode his fiery little horse up to the station platform, and taking off his broad-brimmed hat with a flourish and a bow, asked:

"Is this the moving picture outfit?"

"It is," said Mr. Pertell.

"I reckoned that I'd read your brand right," the cowboy went on. "Welcome to Rocky Ranch!"

"But where is it?" asked Alice, and then she blushed at her own boldness, for the glance of the half-score of cowboys was instantly drawn in her direction, and bold admiration shone in their eyes.

"It isn't far from here, Miss," was the answer. "It lies just over that little rise. You can't see it. We've come to take you out there. That's why we brung the wagons, and some of the boys thought they'd like to ride in and see you, seein' as how the round-up is over and we ain't so terrible rushed with work."

"We heard you coming," said Mr. Pertell. "Some of the ladies were a little apprehensive."

"I don't quite get you," spoke the cowboy.

"I say some of the ladies were a bit timid on account of the firing."

"Oh, shucks! That ain't nothin'! The boys was feelin' a little bit frisky, I reckon, and they maybe did let out a few whoops. But land love you! Mustn't mind a little thing like that. Still, if it's goin' to cause any uneasiness among the females, why I'll tell the boys to cut out all—"

"Oh, no, really we don't mind it!" declared Alice,

impulsively, and again she blushed as the broadside of eyes was trained in her direction.

"Do be quiet!" whispered Ruth. "I don't know what they'll think of you," and she adjusted her dainty lace cuffs, brushing some engine cinders from them.

"I don't care," Alice retorted, "if they're going to be cowboys let them be natural."

The same thought must have been in the mind of Mr. Pertell, for he said:

"Don't put yourselves out on our account, gentlemen. We don't want you to change your ways or customs just because we have come. We want to get moving pictures of the ranch and the cowboys, and we want them true to life. The ladies will soon get used to the firing. We have gone through worse things than that."

"Well, I sure am glad to hear you say so," was the hearty response. "You see it's jest plumb natural for a cow-puncher to shoot off his gun, and it would come a bit hard to stop. But I reckon the boys has had enough for to-day. Now, who's the boss of this outfit?"

"I guess I am," replied Mr. Pertell. "I'll introduce you to the different ones when I get a chance. Just now I think we are all anxious to get to the ranch."

"All right, jest as you say. My name is Batso—Pete Batso, and I'm foreman of Rocky Ranch. The Circle and Dot is our brand—you can see it on the ponies," and he showed on the flank of his mount a circle burned in the hide—a circle in the center of which was a dot. Each ranch owner brands, with a hot iron, all his cattle, that he may pick out his own when

Laura Lee Hope

they mix with another bunch at the grazing. Each ranch has a different brand, and they consist of simple marks and symbols, each one being properly registered in case of lawsuits.

"Now then," went on Foreman Pete, "if you're ready we'll start. The boys will stow away your traps in one of the wagons, and if you'll distribute yourselves in the other wagons we'll git along. I could have brought horses for all of you, but I wasn't sure how many could ride."

"Very few of us do, I'm afraid," observed Mr. Pertell.

"But I'm going to learn!" exclaimed Alice, promptly, and this time, when the eyes were turned toward her, she smiled back at the owners thereof.

"I'll be very pleased to show you how, Miss," declared the foreman, with a low bow to the girl. Alice blushed, and Ruth looked annoyed; but Mr. DeVere smiled indulgently. He understood Alice.

Trunks, valises and the various properties Pop Snooks had provided for the different plays were put in the wagon and then in the other vehicles the players themselves took their places.

"All ready?" asked Pete Batso.

"All ready," answered Mr. Pertell.

"Let her go!" cried the foreman, and the cavalcade started off to the whooping and yelling accompaniment of the cowboys, though this time they did not fire their revolvers.

The pace was fast. In fact, everything out in the West seemed to be fast. No one walked who could, by any means, get a horse, and the horses, or cow ponies, seemed to be always on the trot or gallop when they were not standing still. A slow walk seemed to be the one thing they could not do. Even the teams attached to the wagons were off at the same fast pace.

It was a little breathless at first, but the players soon became used to it, and liked it. The rapid motion made a cooling breeze.

Rocky Ranch was located in a fine part of the country. The land was rolling, with occasional wide, level stretches. About two miles away was a timber belt, through which ran a stream of good water, and about eight miles to the west was a chain of hills, reaching finally into mountains, with an occasional *mesa*, or flat, table-like, isolated hill.

The ranch owner, Mr. Haladay Norton, possessed many cattle, which roamed about his broad acres. There were a number of ranch buildings, and accommodations for all the players, as well as for the necessary help in the line of cowboys. In fact, it was one of the largest and best ranches in that part of the country, which is the reason Mr. Pertell selected it for his purposes.

For some time, as the players rode along with the cowboy escort, they saw no signs of habitation. Off in the distance were dark moving bunches, that the foreman said were some of the Rocky Ranch cattle, and farther off could be seen the foothills.

Then, as the dust blew away, and the cavalcade topped a little rise, they all saw, nestled in a sort of hollow, or swale, a group of red buildings.

"There you are!" cried Pete Batso, pointing with gloved hand toward the collection. "That's Rocky Ranch, and I kin smell supper cookin' right now."

"Some nose you got!" observed a blue-eyed cowboy riding close to the wagon containing Alice and Ruth.

"That's all right, Bow Backus; but I kin, all the same," asserted Pete. "We call him Bow Backus because he's got such crooked legs, from ridin' a horse so much," the foreman explained in a low voice to Mr. DeVere, who sat with his daughters. "Most every cow-puncher gets bow-legged after a while, but Backus is the worst I ever see. You could almost roll a barrel through him when he stands up. That feller next to him is Baldy Johnson," he went on. "His head is like a billiard ball, or an ostrich egg. He's tried all the hair restorers on the market; but they don't do no good. He'll ask you if you ever heard of one he ain't tried, as soon as he gets on speakin' terms with you."

"What odd characters," observed Ruth.

"Aren't they? But delightfully quaint—I like them!" her sister exclaimed.

"Oh, so do I. It's so different from what we've seen. I know we shall have fine times out here."

A little later the cowboy whom the foreman had designated as Baldy Johnson, spurred up beside the wagon in which Mr. Bunn rode. The actor had taken off his hat, and his rather thick and heavy hair was blown about.

"Whoop-ee! Look at that!" cried Baldy, in evident admiration. "I say, no offense, stranger," he went on, "but what brand do you use?"

"Brand?" queried the actor, much puzzled.

"Yes. What sort of stuff do you use on your hair? You've got a fine bunch there. I'd like to get next. Look at me!" and he pulled off his hat and showed a head shiny and bald.

"I—I don't use any," faltered Mr. Bunn, for he saw the cowboy taking a revolver from its holster, and the actor evidently thought he was to be "held up" then and there, and perhaps scalped.

"Too bad. I wish you did, and could tell me what to use," sighed Baldy, and then, with a whoop he raised his gun in the air and fired. Instantly all the other cowboys were doing the same thing, as their horses broke into a fast gallop. Miss Pennington and Miss Dixon screamed, but they need have had no fears, for it was but a repetition of the scene at the station. The cow-punchers were merely celebrating their return to the ranch.

"Glad to see you all," Mr. Norton, the owner, greeted them as he came out to welcome the party. He had met Mr. Pertell in Chicago, where arrangements for the use of the ranch had been made.

Introductions were soon over, and then, under the direction of Mrs. Norton, who proved to be a motherly, home-like sort of person, the ladies of the company were taken to their quarters, and the men shown to theirs.

"You won't find marble halls and electric elevators here," laughed the ranch owner. "In fact, everything's on the ground floor; but you'll find some comforts. I want you to have a good time while you're here. You'll find us a bit rough, perhaps; but you'll find us ready to do our best for you."

"I'm sure of it," agreed Mr. Pertell, heartily.

The players had scarcely removed the dust of travel, and freshened themselves, before the mellow notes of a gong sounded through the air, and at the same time a strident voice cried;

"Glub leady! Glub leady!"

"What in the world is that?" asked Alice.

"That's the Chinese cook, Ling Foo, announcing that grub, or supper, is ready," replied Mr. Norton, with a laugh. "This way to the dining room."

As the company, the members of which were to eat by themselves, filed out, Russ, who was walking beside Mr. Pertell, saw a familiar looking box on a bench.

"Look!" he exclaimed to the manager.

"A moving picture camera!" was the surprised comment. "Is that one of yours left out by mistake?"

"No, mine are in the room with the other props."

"But that's a camera, sure enough, though the lens has been taken off. I wonder how that got here," and he looked anxiously at the young operator.

"I'll ask Mr. Norton," Russ volunteered, and, as the ranch proprietor came along at that moment, Russ had his chance.

"That? Oh, that belongs to a new man I hired the other day," said the ranchman.

"What sort of a man is he?" asked Mr. Pertell, suspiciously.

"Well, not as good a sort as I thought he was. He knows a little about cow-punching; but not much. Still, I was short of help and had to put him on."

"What—what does he do with that?" asked Russ, pointing to the camera out on the bench.

"That? Oh he says that's an electric battery. He uses it for rheumatism; but I haven't seen him work it yet. He said it was out of order, and he's tinkering with it the last few days. Why?"

"Oh, I was just—just wondering," returned Russ, evasively.

Then, as he passed on to the dining room, he saw, through a window, a man hurry up to the bench and remove the camera. Russ could not recall ever having seen this man.

"There's something queer about this," said Mr. Pertell to his operator. "What would a cowboy be doing with a moving picture camera?"

CHAPTER XIII

AT THE BRANDING

Russ did not answer for a moment, but kept on beside the manager through the long corridor that led to the dining hall. Then, just as the two entered the room, Russ said:

"I reckon, as they say out here—I reckon, Mr. Pertell, that you're thinking the same thing I am."

"What's that, Russ?"

"That maybe those International fellows are still on our trail."

"That's what I do think, Russ. Though how they got out here ahead of us is more than I can tell."

"It would be easy enough. They learned we were coming here, and just took a short cut. We've been on the road quite a while."

"That must be it, Russ. But you say you had a glimpse of the fellow who took the camera off the bench. You didn't know him; did you?"

"Never saw him before, as far as I could tell. But there are a lot of camera operators nowadays, so that isn't strange. The International firm could hire anyone and send him on here to try and steal some of the scenes we're depending on. He could pose as a cowboy, too."

"Well, we'll just have to be on our guard, Russ. It won't do to let them get ahead of us. There's too much at stake."

Nothing was said to the players of the suspicions of Russ and Mr. Pertell. They wanted to wait and see what happened.

Though the meal at Rocky Ranch was served without any of the elegance which would have been expected at a hotel, the food was of the best, and there was plenty of it.

"Ah, again sauerkraut!" cried Mr. Switzer, as he saw a steaming dish brought on the table, topped with smoking sausages. "Dot is fine alretty yet!"

"Disgusting!" scoffed Miss Pennington, turning up a nose that in itself showed a tendency to "tilt."

There was time, in the twilight that followed supper, for the players to look about the buildings at Rocky Ranch. All the structures, as Mr. Norton had said, were of only one story. There were broad verandas on most of them and in comfortable chairs one could take one's ease in delightful restfulness.

There was a bunk-house for the cowboys, and a separate living apartment for the Chinese cook and his two assistants, for considerable food was required at Rocky Ranch, especially with the advent of the film players.

The cowboys, their meal over, gathered in a group and

looked curiously at the visitors. The novelty of seeing the pretty girls and the well-dressed men appealed to the rough but sterling chaps who had so little to soften their hard lives.

Nearly every one of them smoked cigarettes, which they rolled skillfully and quickly.

"Give us a song, Buster!" one of the cowboys called to a comrade. "Tune up! Bring out that mouth organ, Necktie!"

"What odd names!" remarked Alice to Pete Batso, who constituted himself a sort of guide to Ruth and her sister.

"They call Dick Jones 'Buster' because he's a good bronco trainer, or buster," the foreman said. "And Necktie Harry got his handle because he's so fussy about his ties. I'll wager he's got *three*, all different," and the foreman seemed to think that a great number.

"You should see our Mr. Towne," laughed Paul, who had joined the girls. "I guess he must have thirty!"

"Thirty!" cried Pete. "What is he—a wholesale dealer?"

"Pretty nearly," admitted Paul.

"Say, Pete!" called one of the cowboys, "can't some of them actor folks do a song and dance?"

The foreman looked questioningly at Alice, with whom he was already on friendly terms because of her happy frankness.

"I'm afraid that isn't in our line," she said.

"I'll do that little sketch I did with Miss Pennington and Miss

Dixon," offered Paul, who had been in vaudeville. "I've got my banjo and—"

"Ki-yi, fellows! We're going to have a show!" yelled Bow Backus. "Come on!" and he fired his revolver in the air.

Ruth jumped nervously.

"Here, cut that out!" ordered the foreman to the offending cowboy. "Save your powder to mill the cattle."

"I begs your pardon, Miss," said the cowboy, humbly. "But I jest couldn't help it—thinkin' we was goin' to have a little amusement. It's been powerful dull out here lately. Nothin' to do but shoot the queue off Ling Foo."

"Oh! you don't do that; do you?" gasped Ruth.

"Don't mind him, Miss," said the foreman, "he's jokin'."

Miss Pennington and Miss Dixon were only too willing to show their talents to the appreciative audience of cowboys, and with Paul, who played the banjo, they went through the little sketch, with a side porch as a stage, and the setting sun as a spotlight.

There were ample sleeping quarters at Rocky Ranch, though the bedrooms were rather of the camp, or bungalow, type. But there was hot and cold water and this made up for the lack of many other things.

"Do you think you're going to like it here, Alice?" asked Ruth as they sat in the room they were to share. Ruth was manicuring her nails, and Alice was combing her hair.

"Like it? Of course I'm going to like it. Aren't you?"

Laura Lee Hope

"Well, it's—er—rather—rough," she hesitated.

"Oh, but it's all so real! There's no sham about anything. They take you for just what you are worth out here, and not a cent more. There's no sham!"

"No, that's true. But everything seems so—so different."

"I know—there isn't romance enough for you. You'd like a horseman to wear a suit of armor, or come prancing up in a top hat and shiny boots. But these men, in their rough clothes and on their scraggy-looking ponies, can *ride*. I saw some of them just before supper. They can ride like the wind and pull up so short that it's a wonder they don't turn somersaults. I'm going to learn to ride that way."

"Alice, you're not!"

"Well, maybe not so well, of course," the younger girl admitted, as she finished braiding her hair for the night. "But I'm going to learn. I'll have to, anyhow, as I'm cast for a riding part in several scenes, and so are you."

"Well, then, I suppose I'll have to. But I hope I will get a gentle horse."

"Oh, Pete will see to that."

"Pete? Do you call him by his first name so soon?" asked Ruth rather shocked, as she shook out her robe, and ran a ribbon through the neck.

"Everyone calls him Pete; why shouldn't I?" laughed Alice. "He's awfully nice—and he's been married three times!"

"Did you ask him that?"

"No, he told me. He asked me if I'd ever been 'hooked up,' as he called it."

"Alice DeVere!"

"Well, I couldn't help it. He meant all right. He's old enough to be our father. Do you think daddy is quite well?" she asked, perhaps to change the subject.

"Yes, I think the pure air out here is doing him good. His throat seems much improved. Are those my slippers?" she asked, quickly, as Alice thrust her pink feet into a pair of worsted "tootsies."

"Indeed they are not. I just took these out of my trunk. There are yours under your bed."

"Oh, excuse me. I don't believe I shall need anyone to sing me to sleep to-night," and she yawned comfortably.

There were to be busy times at Rocky Ranch next day, for some cattle were to be branded, or marked with the hot iron to establish their ownership, and Mr. Pertell had decided to have some scenes of this, with his own players worked in as part of the action.

This had already been planned, and after breakfast there was a short rehearsal of the players, while the cowboys were getting ready for the branding.

"Now we're ready for you," announced Pete Batso, who was in charge of the cowboys. "Get your players in position. They're going to rope the first critter now."

The proper action for the scene was gone through by Ruth, Alice, Paul and Mr. Sneed, and then one of the cowboys "cut out," or separated from the rest, a young steer that had not yet been branded.

"Whoop-ee!" yelled the cow puncher as he hurled his lariat and pulled the animal to the ground. Other cowboys quickly threw their ropes around the fore and hind legs of the steer and then, with another rope around the head, the creature was stretched out helpless, ready for the application of the iron.

CHAPTER XIV

A WARNING

"Oh, doesn't it hurt them?" faltered Ruth, as creature after creature was branded.

"No, Miss, hardly at all," Pete Batso assured her. "You see they're used to being roped, and we don't throw them as hard as it looks, onless it's an ornery critter that wants to make trouble. And the hot iron doesn't go in deep. It just sort of crimples up the hair, same as you ladies frizzes your curls with a hot slate pencil—at least my second wife—no, it was my third—she used to curl hers that way."

Ruth had difficulty to keep from laughing.

The branding was almost over, and the taking of pictures was nearly at an end. Russ had obtained some good films, and the action was spirited.

"Here comes a bad one," announced the foreman, as the cow punchers cut out from the herd a big steer. "That's a vicious critter, all right!"

"Oh, is there any danger?" asked Alice, for she and Ruth had finished their work. Mr. Bunn and Paul were engaged in the

Laura Lee Hope

final scenes, not far from the place of the branding.

"Oh, don't worry. That critter won't get away from the boys," the foreman assured her. "It's a steer that some of the other ranchmen around here tried to claim for theirs. They changed the brand by burnin' an arrow over our circle and dot. Now we've got to put our brand on again. The steer knows what's comin', I guess."

Indeed the animal did, for it resisted, for some time, the efforts of the cowboys to separate it from the rest of the bunch. But finally it was forced out into an open space, and there quickly roped and thrown.

"Lively now, boys!" called the foreman. "We've got to clear out of here right after this, and look after that bunch of critters by Sweetwater Brook. I hear the rustlers have been after them. So get a move on."

"What are rustlers?" asked Alice, who seldom let pass a chance to acquire information.

"Cattle stealers, Miss. Ornery, mean men who trade on the rights of others. But we'll snub 'em if we get hold of 'em!"

The branding of the big steer was quickly done and then the restraining ropes were cast off so that it might get up. With a deep bellow the animal sprang to its feet. It stood still for a moment and then, with a snort, it wheeled around and made straight for Mr. Bunn.

For a moment the veteran actor stood still. Fortunately, some little distance separated him from the steer. Otherwise he might have been impaled on its short horns.

"Run! Run!" cried Pete Batso. "Get out the way, and give the boys a chance to rope him!"

Mr. Bunn needed no second call. He sprang to one side, in time to avoid a sweep of the horns, and started to run. The steer, evidently connecting the actor with the recent branding, made after him, and then began a chase that might have resulted seriously.

"Stop him! Save me! Do something!" cried Mr. Bunn, as he raced about, keeping just ahead of the angry steer.

"Just a minute—we'll rope him!" cried the foreman. But the trouble was that the cowboys nearest the scene had just pulled their lariat from the branded beast and the ropes were not coiled in readiness for throwing. The foreman himself had left his at the ranch house.

On rushed Mr. Bunn. On came the steer, and only a little way behind the actor. The distance was lessening every second.

"He ought to be on a horse—then he wouldn't have any trouble," declared the foreman. "Lively there, Buster—get that critter!"

"Right away, Pete," was the answer as the cowboy coiled his rope for a throw. Then, galloping his pony up behind the steer, Buster threw the lariat over the head of the animal, and brought it with a thud to the ground.

"Oh, am I safe?" gasped Mr. Bunn as he sank down on some saddles that had been removed from the horses.

"You're all right now," Paul assured him. "But it certainly was a lively time while it lasted."

"That's so," agreed Russ, who had not deserted his camera. "But why didn't you run toward me while you were at it. I could have made better pictures then."

"Do you—do you mean to say you took a film of me running away from that—that cow?" panted Mr. Bunn, who had lost his tall silk hat early in the chase.

"Well, I just couldn't help it," confessed Russ. "It was too good to miss. I think I got most of it."

"Where's Mr. Pertell?" demanded Mr. Bunn, getting up quickly. "I want to see the manager at once."

"What's the trouble?" asked that gentleman, as he came up.

"I demand that you destroy that film of me being chase by a cow!" cried Mr. Bunn. "I shall be the laughing stock of all the moving picture theaters of the United States. I demand that that film be not shown. To be chased by a *cow*!"

"But it wasn't a cow, my friend," spoke the foreman. "It was a vicious steer and you might have been badly hurt if Buster hadn't roped it in time."

"Is that so?" asked Mr. Bunn.

"It sure is!"

"Well, er—then—perhaps after all, if it was as important as that, you may show the film," conceded the Shakespearean actor, who had a large idea of his own importance. "We might make it into some sort of a play like 'Quo Vadis?'" he went on.

"Hardly," said Mr. Pertell with a smile. "They didn't wear tall silk hats in those days. But I'll change the script of this play to conform to the chase. I'm glad you were not hurt, Mr. Bunn."

"So am I. I thought several times that I felt those horns in my back."

The vicious steer was held by the ropes until the company of players had left the scene. Then it was allowed to get up and join the rest of the bunch. By that time it seemed to have lost all desire to attack.

"Sometimes a steer will come for a person that isn't on horseback," explained Pete Batso. "You see, the cattle are so used to seeing mounted men that they can't get used to anyone afoot. You want to get your players mounted," he added to Mr. Pertell, who was a fair horseman, and who was on this occasion in the saddle.

"I guess I will," agreed the manager. "Some of the young ladies are quite anxious to try it, if you have some gentle mounts."

"Oh, I think I can fix them up. My boys will quarrel among themselves, though, for the privilege of giving lessons to 'em. You see we don't get much of ladies' society out here and we appreciate it so much the more."

"I see," laughed Mr. Pertell.

The next few days were given over to horseback practice on the part of all the members of the moving picture company save Mrs. Maguire. She declared she was too old to learn, and as she would not be required in mounted scenes she was excused. But her little grandchildren were provided with gentle ponies and taught how to sit in the saddle. Mr. DeVere had ridden in his youth, and the knack of it soon came back to him, though he was a trifle heavy. Paul took to it naturally, and Miss Pennington and Miss Dixon were soon able to hold their own, as was Ruth.

But Alice was the "star," according to Baldy Johnson, who insisted on being her instructor. She was an apt pupil, and he was a good and conscientious teacher. In less than a week Alice was very sure of herself in the saddle.

"Oh, it's simply great! It's wonderful!" she cried as she came back one day from a gallop, with red cheeks and eyes that sparkled with the light of health and life. "I wouldn't have missed it for anything!"

"I am glad you like it," said her father. "It is good exercise for you."

"I like it, too," declared Ruth, "but I'm not as keen for it as Alice is."

"Oh, I just love it!" cried the younger girl, enthusiastically.

"Now we'll begin some real Western scenes, since you can all ride fairly well," remarked Mr. Pertell.

"Fairly well—huh! She's a peach at it—that's what she is—a peach!" cried Baldy Johnson, with a look of admiration at his pupil. Alice blushed with delight.

During the days of horseback practice Mr. Pertell and Russ had been on the lookout for any signs of activity on the part of their rivals in the moving picture business; but nothing had happened. The man with the other camera seemed to have disappeared.

"Maybe they've given up," suggested Russ.

"I hope so," agreed Mr. Pertell.

A few days later several important scenes were to be filmed, and one evening Alice, who was to have a large share in the acting, had her horse saddled, and with Ruth and her father, accompanied by Baldy, set off for a little gallop.

"Let's go over to that *mesa*," suggested Alice, pointing to a big, elevated hill, standing boldly and abruptly upright in the midst of the plain.

"No, I wouldn't go there," said Baldy, flicking his horse with the reins. "That's a dangerous place, Miss. Best keep away."

CHAPTER XV

THE INDIAN RITES

Alice glanced curiously at the cowboy. There seemed to be a strange look on his face.

"What do you mean?" she asked, adding in a half-bantering tone: "Is it haunted?"

"Oh, Alice!" objected Ruth, shaking out her skirt so it would hang down a little longer, for the girls rode side-saddle.

"No, Miss, it ain't exactly haunted," replied Baldy. "But it ain't a safe place to go—least-ways, not all alone."

"But why?" persisted Alice.

"Because that's a sort of sacred place—at least some of the Indians from the reservation think so—and, though it's off their land, and really belongs to Mr. Norton, them redskins come over, once in a while, to hold some of their heathen rites on it."

"Oh, how interesting!" the girl cried. "I wonder if we couldn't see them? Do they do a snake dance, and things like that?"

"Well, yes, in a way," Baldy admitted. "But it ain't safe to go watch 'em. Them Indians are peculiar. They don't want strangers lookin' on, and more than once they've made trouble when outsiders tried to climb up there and watch. As I said, the Indians come from their reservation, which is several miles away, to that place for their ceremonies. And they come at odd times, so there's no tellin' when you might strike a body of 'em up on top there, pow-wowin' to beat the band, and yellin' fit to split your ears. So it's best to keep away."

"Are the Indians really dangerous?" asked Mr. DeVere.

"Well, I don't s'pose they'd actually *scalp* you," replied Baldy, slowly.

"Oh, how terrible!" exclaimed Ruth with a shiver.

"They ain't got no right to come off their reservation," went on the cowboy; "but they do it all the same. You see this place is pretty well out of the way, and by the time we could get troops here to drive 'em back, they'd probably be gone of their own accord, anyhow. So we sort of let 'em alone. They don't bother us, and we don't bother them. Just keep away from that hill, that's all, for it's so high you can't see the top of it unless you climb up, and there's no tellin' when the Indians come and go."

"I should like to see some of those rites, just the same," declared Alice.

"Oh, but you won't go there; will you?" begged Ruth. "Promise me you won't, my dear. Daddy, make her!"

"I won't go *alone*, I promise you that," laughed Alice.

"Of course with a party it might be all right," assented Baldy, "but even then the Indians act rather hostile."

"Mr. Pertell will be sure to want some moving pictures of the Indians, if he hears about them," said Mr. DeVere. "Better not tell him, or he might run into danger—or send Russ."

"Then we won't say a thing about it!" exclaimed Ruth, with such sudden energy that Alice laughed.

"Oh, no, we mustn't endanger *Russ*!" she said, mockingly.

"Alice!" exclaimed Ruth, with gentle dignity, her face the while being suffused with a burning blush. "I meant I didn't want *anyone* to run into danger."

"I understand, my dear. Oh, but isn't that sunset gorgeous?— to change the subject," and she laughed at the serious expression on Ruth's face.

The scene was indeed beautiful. The *mesa* seemed to be suffused by a purple glow, while, farther off, the foothills, from which it was separated by a level expanse, were in a golden haze. The *mesa* stood up boldly, almost like some giant toadstool, save that the stem was thicker. There was an overhang to the top, or table part, though, that carried out the resemblance.

"I should think that would be difficult of access," observed Mr. DeVere.

"There's an easy way up on the other side," returned Baldy. "The Indians always use that side. It's a narrow path to the top."

The cowboys, their work over for the day, were indulging in

some of their pastimes—rough riding, feats in throwing the lariat, jumping, wrestling and the like.

"Don't you want to go with them?" asked Alice of their escort.

"No, Miss, I—I'd rather be with you," Baldy replied, simply, but he blushed even under his coat of tan.

"Now who's to blame?" asked Ruth in a low voice of her sister, as she regarded her with a quizzical smile.

"I can't help it if he likes me," murmured the younger girl.

In fact both Ruth and Alice were favorites with all the cowboys, who were always willing to perform any little service for them. The other members of the moving picture company, too, were well liked; but Ruth and Alice seemed to come first. Perhaps it was because they were both so natural and girlish, and took such an interest in the life and doings at Rocky Ranch.

Ruth and Alice were fast becoming adepts in the saddle. The other members of the company, too, soon felt more at home on the back of a horse, and Mr. Pertell allowed them to rehearse in the scenes where mounted action was necessary.

Mr. Bunn had one rather unlucky experience on a horse, and for some time after that he refused to mount a steed, even going to the length of threatening to resign if compelled to.

The "old school" actor was rather supercilious in his manner, and this was resented by some of the cowboys, who thought him "stuck up." They therefore planned a little joke on him. At least, it was a joke to them.

The horse Mr. Bunn had learned to ride was a steady-going beast that had outlived its frisky days, and plodded along just the pace that suited the actor. But there was, among the ranch animals, a "bucking bronco," who looked so much like Mr. Bunn's horse that even some of the cowboys had difficulty in telling them apart.

A bucking bronco, it might be explained, is a steed who by nature or training uses every means in its power to unseat its rider. The bucking consists in the horse leaping into the air, with all four feet off the ground, and coming down stiff-legged, jarring to a considerable degree the person in the saddle.

One day, just for a "joke," the bucking bronco was brought out for Mr. Bunn to ride, when a certain film was to be made. He did not notice that it was not his regular mount. The bronco was quiet and tractable enough until Mr. Bunn settled himself in the saddle, and then, just as Russ was about to make the film, the pony set off at a fast pace.

"Whoa, there! Whoa!" cried Mr. Bunn, trying to halt the beast, and not understanding what could have gotten into his usually quiet mount. "Whoa, there!"

"Give him a touch of the spur," called the mischievous cowboy.

Mr. Pertell did not know what to make of the actions of his actor, for the play called for nothing like that.

"Shall I get that?" asked Russ, and before the manager could answer the bronco began running around in a circle.

"Yes! Get it!" ordered Mr. Pertell. "We can change the play to work it in. It's too funny to lose."

"Whoa! Stop it! Somebody stop him! I'm getting dizzy!" cried Mr. Bunn, leaning forward and clasping his arms about the neck of the pony.

By accident he dug the spurs lightly into the side of the beast, and as this always made the animal buck, or leap up into the air, it now changed its tactics.

With legs held stiff it rose several feet, and came down hard. Mr. Bunn was bounced up, and would have been bounced off had he not had that neck grip. Again the bronco bucked.

"Oh stop him! Stop him!" cried the actor.

"Get every move of that, Russ!" called Mr. Pertell.

But there was not much more to get, for with the next buck Mr. Bunn's hold was loosened and away he shot, out of the saddle. Fortunately he landed on a pile of hay and was not hurt beyond a shaking up. But Russ got a good picture of the whole scene. The actor picked himself up, and without a word started for the ranch house. Probably he suspected the trick that had been played on him, and for some days after that he refused to mount a horse, so Mr. Pertell had to make some changes in his plans, as he did not care to antagonize Mr. Bunn by insisting on his taking part.

And when the actor did again get into the saddle, he had his horse branded on one hoof, as army horses are marked, so he could not again be deceived.

Life at Rocky Ranch was a delight to all the moving picture players, though there was plenty of hard work, too.

Of course it was impossible to keep from Mr. Pertell the story of the Indians and their rites on the *mesa*, and he determined, before he left the West, to get a film of them.

"But you'll have to be careful, Russ, how you go about it," he said.

"That's what I will," agreed the operator.

It was about a week after this that Russ, Paul, Alice, Ruth and Mr. DeVere were riding out toward the *mesa* to get some scenes in the foothills, the two girls, their father and Paul being scheduled to go through a little act by themselves.

As they passed under the shadow of the eminence Russ looked up and saw a thin wisp of smoke curling around the top.

"Look!" he exclaimed. "I wonder if the Indians can be there now, doing some of their snake ceremonies?"

"Let's have a look," suggested Paul. "We've got lots of time. I'd like to have a peep."

"I would too!" exclaimed Alice.

"Oh, Daddy, will it be safe?" asked Ruth, for she saw that her father seemed interested.

"There are so many of us, I think so," he replied. "We will try it, at all events. They can no more than tell us to go. I should very much like to see what they do, and perhaps I can get some of their weapons or musical instruments for my collection," for the actor had that fad. And then, though Ruth was a bit timid about it, they turned toward the elevated table land to see if the Indians were at their rites.

CHAPTER XVI

PRISONERS

"Russ, are you going to try to get a film?" asked Alice, as she saw the young operator examining his camera.

"I was thinking of it," he confessed. "I guess I've got film enough to get you people, and take about eight hundred feet of the Indians—that is, if they'll let us."

"Maybe we can make them believe the camera is some new kind of magic, that will help them better than some of their own," suggested Paul. "One of the cowboys was telling me the Indians come here to make magic or 'medicine' that they take back to the reservation with them, to ward off sickness, bring good crops, and the like."

"Well, don't run into danger, whatever you do," advised Mr. DeVere. "We'll just take a look, if we can, and come away."

"But I want a film," insisted Russ.

They were nearing the *mesa*. The smoke on top was seen to be growing thicker, but there were no other signs that the Indians were on top of the peculiar, table-like formation.

"Suppose they aren't there?" suggested Paul.

"Oh, don't come any of that Mr. Sneed business," laughed Russ. "Don't cross a bridge until you come to it. I guess they're there, all right."

"Who's that coming after us?" asked Ruth, as she turned in her saddle, and indicated an approaching horseman, who was coming on at a gallop. A cloud of dust almost hid him, and it could not be made out who he was.

A little later, as he drew nearer, however, he was seen to be Baldy Johnson. He waved his hat at them, his bald pate shining in the hot sun, and called out:

"Hold on! Where you goin'?"

"Up to the *mesa*," answered Russ. "The Indians are there, I think, and we want to see them. I want to get some pictures."

The two girls expected Baldy to make an objection, but he merely said:

"Well, I guess it'll be safe enough this time. I'll go along with you. There's only a small party of them up there now."

"Then you know the Indians are there?" asked Alice.

"Yes, we got word at the ranch last night that they were on the way for one of their regular pow-wows. One of the boys was out looking up some stray cattle and he seen 'em headin' for the *mesa*. But there wasn't many, so I guess it'll be safe. I'll go along," and he glanced significantly at the two big revolvers that hung from either hip.

"But can you spare the time?" asked Alice.

"Oh, yes, Miss. I'd make time, anyhow," and he smiled frankly at her. That was one nice feature of Baldy's admiration. It was so open and ingenuous that no one—not even Ruth—could take offense at it. "I'm on a little round-up of my own, looking for signs of rustlers, and I haven't any special office hours," he finished, laughingly. "So come along. I'll take you by the easiest path."

The ride around the *mesa*, to a point where it could be climbed, took nearly an hour. During that time the girls and the others cast curious glances at the top of the table-like elevation, but were not able to detect any signs of the redmen. The little pillar of smoke, too, disappeared.

"Now for some hard work; but take it as easy as you can," suggested Baldy, as they came to the trail that led up the slope.

"Oh, we can never get the horses up that," objected Ruth, as she looked at the elevation. "It's too steep."

"Just leave it to the ponies, Miss," responded Baldy. "They know how to make it easy for themselves and you. Leave it to them. I'll take the lead, and you follow me. Take it easy!"

It was not as difficult as it looked, once the horses were given free rein. Baldy's pony seemed to have traveled the trail before and, on inquiry, the girls learned that this was so.

"When I'm sure I'm not goin' to run into a bunch of redskins I often come up here," said the cowboy. "I can get a good view of the country from this elevation, when I'm trying to locate a strayed bunch of cattle."

"Isn't it lonesome here?" asked Ruth, as she looked about her, and up and down the trail. Indeed the scenery was wild and desolate, though imposing in its grandeur.

"Well, it ain't exactly the 'Great White Way' that Miss Pennington and Miss Dixon talk so much about," chuckled Baldy. "There ain't no skyscrapers except the *mesa* itself, and there's no electric lights."

"But I like it, just the same!" cried Alice, impulsively. "I think it's just great! This is the finest country in the world!"

"It sure is, Miss," agreed Baldy in a low voice. "The Lord didn't make a better," he added, reverently.

The trail became easier for a time, and then more difficult until, as they neared the top, the girls were almost ready to give up and go back. Mr. DeVere, too, was a little doubtful about continuing.

"Suppose they drive us back?" the actor asked. "We would never be able to negotiate a retreat safely down such a slope."

"Oh, I guess it's all right this time," said Baldy. "But if it wasn't that I'm sure there are only a few Indians here, I wouldn't have let you come. Keep on. I guess you'll be all right."

By dint of struggling the ponies covered the short remaining distance and, a little later, the party found itself on the summit. They were among a lot of stunted trees and straggling bushes, on top of the flat expanse that stood so high above the surrounding country.

"Oh, what a view!" cried Alice, as she looked off to the west, toward the foothills and mountains.

"Isn't it?" agreed Ruth. "I wouldn't have missed it for anything."

"But where are the Indians?" asked Russ, who was getting his moving picture machine ready for work.

"Oh, they're probably somewhere in the middle of the place," said Baldy. "It's about three miles across it, you know."

They gave the horses a breathing spell, and then started slowly across the table land. There was no smoke in sight now, and as far as could be told from observation, they were alone on the plateau.

"It's likely the Indians are getting ready to make their 'medicine,'" said Baldy. "Now leave everything to me. I can speak some of their lingo, so I'll do the talking. I'll tell 'em you have powerful 'medicine' in that picture machine of yours," he went on to Russ. "That may stop them from taking a notion to throw stones at it."

"Would they do that?" asked the young operator.

"Oh, they might—there's not much counting on what an Indian will do, especially at these ceremonies. But I'll fix it all right. Just leave it to me."

Though the top of the *mesa* was flat, it was only comparatively so. There were little hollows and ridges, and when the riders were down in some of the depressions they could not see very far ahead.

They kept on, becoming more and more impressed with the wonderful view. It was a new experience for the Easterners, and they appreciated it.

"I guess it's going to turn out a false alarm," Russ observed, as he shifted the weight of his camera.

"No, they're here," returned Baldy, in a low voice.

"How can you tell?" Alice asked.

"I can hear the stamping of their ponies. They're tethered just beyond there—past that clump of trees." He pointed as he spoke, and, at the same moment, from that direction came the whinny of a pony. It was answered by Baldy's horse.

"I thought so," said the cowboy, quietly. "They're here."

"Good enough!" declared Russ. "Mr. Pertell will be pleased to get this film."

"You haven't got it—yet," remarked Paul, significantly.

A little later they passed along a trail that led to a grove of small trees, where a score or more of Indian ponies were tied. But of the Indians themselves not a sign was to be seen.

"Where are they?" asked Alice.

"You'll soon find out," was Baldy's reply. "They're most likely in their huts. They'll mine out in a minute."

As he spoke they emerged from the clump of trees that served as a stable, and there, in an open space, were nearly a hundred rude huts, made of tree branches roughly twined together. Over some of them were cowhides, tanned with hair on, while others were covered with gaudy blankets.

"There's where they stay while the ceremonies are going on," spoke Baldy. "They're all in the huts now, probably, watching us."

He had hardly finished before there were loud cries, and from the huts poured a motley gathering of Indians. They were attired in very scant costumes—in fact, they were as near like the aborigines as is customary in these modern days. And most of them had, streaked on their faces and bodies, colored earth or fire-ashes. Crude, fierce, and rather terrifying were these painted Indians.

"Oh!" faltered Ruth, as the savages advanced toward them.

"Now don't be a bit skeered, Miss," said Baldy, calmly. "I'll palaver to 'em, and tell 'em we just come to pay 'em a visit."

One Indian, taller and better looking than any of the others, stepped out in advance and came close to the party of players, who had halted their horses.

He spoke in short, quick, guttural tones, and looked from one to the other, as if asking who was the spokesman.

"I'll talk to you," said Baldy, and then he lapsed into the Indian dialect. The two talked for a little while, and it was evident that some dispute was taking place.

At first, however, the voices were kept down, and each of the talkers was calm. Then something the Indian said seemed to annoy Baldy.

"Well, you just try it on, and see what happens!" cried the cowboy, hotly. "If you think we're afraid of you it's a big mistake," and, whether unconsciously or not, his hand slid toward the weapon on his right hip.

"What is the trouble? Are we not welcome here?" asked Mr.

DeVere. "If so—"

"Oh, they don't so much mind our coming, as I told 'em we had rights here," replied Baldy. "But the trouble is they don't want us to go until their ceremonies are over. They say it will spoil the magic if we come and go so quickly, so they want to keep us here a couple of days."

"As prisoners?" asked Paul, quickly.

"That's about it," was the cowboy's laconic answer.

CHAPTER XVII

THE RESCUE

Ruth and Alice gasped convulsively, and then urged their horses nearer to their father's mount. Russ and Paul looked curiously, and a bit apprehensively, at each other. As for Baldy, he sat confronting the tall, thin Indian who had announced the ultimatum of his tribe.

"What are you going to do?" asked Russ of the cowboy.

"Will we have to stay here?" Paul wanted to know.

"Oh, that would be impossible," objected Mr. DeVere. "I would not allow my daughters to remain out over night."

Baldy moved uneasily in his saddle.

"I sort of got you into this trouble," he said, apologetically, "and I guess I'll have to get you out. We'll have a talk among ourselves," he went on. "Some of these fellows understand English, and it's just as well to be on the safe side."

Then, turning to the Indian, Baldy said:

"We go for pow-wow!"

"Ugh!" was the answer. The Indian then made a sign to his followers, at the same time calling something to them in a high-pitched voice.

"What is he saying?" asked Alice, as she and the others moved off to one side.

"He's postin' guard so we can't sneak off, and go down to the plain again," explained Baldy. "There's only one way off, and that's the way we came. He's going to guard that way."

"Oh!" cried Ruth, apprehensively.

"Now don't you go to worrying, little girl," said Baldy, quickly. "This will come out all right. I got you into this mess, and I'll get you out. There's a bigger band of the Injuns than I calculated on, though," he added, ruefully, "and they're not in the best of tempers, either."

"Is—er—is there any real danger?" ventured Mr. DeVere.

"No, I'm sure they won't do anything rash, even if they insist on keepin' us here until their ceremonies are over," replied Baldy. "But they won't do that, if I can help it."

Some of the Indians went back into the huts, where they had apparently been resting in preparation for the coming rites. Others moved off toward the grove where the horses were tethered, evidently to mount guard against the escape of their prisoners. Then the chief, if such he was, went into a hut that stood apart from the others.

Baldy led his friends to a secluded place, under the shade of a clump of stunted trees, and then, after carefully looking about, to make sure there were no listening Indians, he said:

"Now we'll consider what's best to do!"

"Would it be safe to do anything—I mean to try to get away by force?" asked Mr. DeVere. "I certainly don't like the idea of being held a prisoner by these Indians."

"Neither do I," agreed Baldy. "It's the first time one of 'em ever got the best of me, and I don't like it. Now I tried to talk strong to him at first, and told him his crowd would get in all kinds of hot water if they held us here."

"What did he say?" asked Russ.

"He didn't seem much impressed by my line of talk," confessed Baldy. "He said this ceremony was one of the most important the tribe ever held, and that it would certainly spoil it to have us go away now. He doesn't want us here, and he says we mustn't be present at the time the magic medicine is made; but, at the same time, he doesn't want us to go."

"That's strange," observed Alice.

"Well, you can't tell much about Indians," Baldy went on. "They are mostly queer critters, anyhow. Now, the question is: Do you want me to go out there, and shoot 'em up, and—"

"No, never!" cried Ruth. "You—you might be hurt."

"Well, yes, there's a possibility of that," returned Baldy, calmly. "But I reckon I could hurt a few of them at the same time. But it's bound to muss things up any way you look at it. Though I might be able to clear out enough of 'em so the others wouldn't bother you. I'm a pretty good shot."

"No, we must not think of that," declared Mr. DeVere, positively. "That is too much of a risk for you, my dear sir. We will try some other line of argument. If we make it plain that they will be punished for detaining us perhaps they will think better of it."

"Well, I'll give them another line of strong talk, and see what comes of it," agreed Baldy. "I'll point out the error of their ways to them."

"Tell them we can't—we simply can't—stay all night," said Ruth, nervously pulling at her gauntlets. "Why, where could we sleep, and what could we eat?"

"We brought along some sandwiches," Alice reminded her.

"Yes, my dear, I know. But hardly enough, and as for sleeping with those—those Indians about—Oh, I couldn't shut my eyes all night. Please, Baldy, tell them we *must* be let go."

"I'll do my best," he responded. "But old Jumping Horse— that's the chief—said we could have some huts off by ourselves, and they'll feed us—such fodder as they've got."

"It is an unfortunate situation," said Mr. DeVere, "but it cannot be helped. We must make the best of it, and, after all, I suppose there is really no great danger."

"None at all, I guess, if we do as they say," agreed Baldy. "But I don't fancy being kept here a week."

"Do their ceremonies last as long as that?" asked Russ.

"Often longer. Well, I'll go see what I can do, and then I'll come back and report. Here, you keep one of those," and he handed a big revolver to Paul.

"Don't you dare hold that close to me!" cried Ruth, apprehensively.

The result of Baldy's talk with Jumping Horse was not encouraging, as the cowboy reported later.

"You can't argue with an Indian," he said, gloomily. "He can only see his side of the game."

"Then he refuses to let us go?" asked Mr. DeVere.

"That's about it," was the moody answer. "He says we won't be bothered; that we can have some huts to ourselves, away from the others, and that we can have the best food they've got. Fortunately they came prepared for a feast and as they've got mostly store victuals it may not be so bad."

"Then you advise submitting quietly?" asked Mr. DeVere.

"For a time, anyhow," replied Baldy. "But I haven't played all my hand yet. I'm going to try and get away, or else bring a rescue party from the ranch."

"How can you do that?" asked Russ.

"Well, I've got to plan it out. Now, of course I'm willin', as it was my fault for bringin' you here—I'm willin' to go out and try to break through their line of guards, if you say so."

"Oh, no!" cried Alice. "Besides, it was as much our doing in coming here as it was yours."

"Certainly," agreed her father. "Don't think of it, my dear sir! Don't think of it!"

"Then we'll be as satisfied as we can," concluded Baldy.

"And maybe to-night, when they're at their ceremonies, we can sneak off."

They agreed this was the best plan under the circumstances, and a little later they were led by two or three Indians to a collection of huts that seemed larger and cleaner than the others. A supply of food was also brought for the prisoners, and, as it consisted largely of canned stuff, that was clean also.

The huts, which were really quite substantial wigwams, were apportioned among the prisoners. Ruth and Alice received the largest and best one, and their father had one by himself next to theirs. Paul and Russ "bunked" together, for Baldy said he wanted to be free to come and go as he liked.

"I'll have to be on the watch," he said.

"What's that big open place over there?" asked Russ, pointing to a level, sandy circle surrounded by small huts.

"That's where they have all the rites and ceremonies," explained Baldy.

"Then that's just what I want!" went on Russ, with enthusiasm. "I can poke a hole in the side of our hut, stick the lens of the camera through, and get moving pictures of the whole business. That will be great!"

"There is nothing but what seems to have some compensations," observed Alice, in her droll way.

Left to themselves, though doubtless they were closely watched by the Indians, the prisoners made ready for their stay. They had brought along a number of blankets, for they were to have been used in taking pictures of the scenes of one of the dramas. Now the coverings would come in very nicely if they were obliged to remain all night.

"Well, let's eat," suggested Baldy. "It's most noon, and I'm hungry."

"So am I," confessed Alice.

It was not a very "nice" meal, but it was very satisfying, and certainly everyone had a good appetite.

The tin cans served as dishes, and their fingers were knives and forks. Baldy carried on his saddle a simple camping outfit, one item of which was a coffee pot, with a supply of the ground berry, and, making a little fire, he soon had some prepared. They all felt better after that.

Directly after noon the Indians went through some of their ceremonies. They circled about the sandy place, to the accompaniment of wild and weird yells, cavorting and dancing, weaving in and out and shaking all manner of noisemaking contrivances. A fire was built in the center of the circle, and there appeared to be some sort of sacrifice going on at a rude stone altar.

Russ, with his camera concealed in a hut, got a fine series of moving pictures of all that went on. Then came more dancing and wild howling, all meaningless to the prisoners, but doubtless of moment to the Indians.

"Oh, that one is doing a regular hesitation waltz!" cried Alice, pointing to a tall, lank brave.

"How can you say such things—at a time like this?" Ruth demanded.

"Why shouldn't I? Besides I've got an idea for a new step in the hesitation from him. I'm going to practice as soon as I get back."

All that afternoon the ceremonies kept up. At one time it seemed as though the Indians would go wild, so frenzied did they become, and Baldy thought it would be a good chance to see if he could not get past the guards with his friends.

But when he reached the trail that led off the *mesa* he found it closely guarded, and he was ordered back.

"No use," he said on his return. "We'll have to wait until night."

But at night he succeeded no better, for though the ceremonies were kept up by the light of many camp fires, the line of Indians on guard was not broken, and it was impossible to get through it.

"We'll just have to stay," announced Baldy.

Ruth cried a little, and even Alice felt a bit gloomy as the shadows settled down when the watch fires died out. But then their father was with them, and he did not seem at all despondent, so their spirits rose.

"This experience will be something to talk about afterward," Mr. DeVere told them.

During the night, when all seemed quiet, Baldy made another attempt, hoping he and his friends could get away, by leaving their horses behind. But the guards were on the alert.

The night was not a comfortable one, and no one slept much; but the huts and blankets were a protection. The Indians did not come near their prisoners, and in the morning they furnished them food.

Baldy tried again to argue with Jumping Horse and some of the others, but it was useless. To all the cowboy's arguments, and even threats, the reply was that if the prisoners left before the ceremonies were over all the medicine and magic would be spoiled.

"We'll have to stay, then," sighed Mr. DeVere. "But it will be out of the question to remain a week—and you say that it will take that long?"

"Yes," answered Baldy.

"Help may come from the ranch before then," suggested Russ.

"It will if I can do what I have in mind," declared Baldy, as he watched a column of smoke ascending from the fire he had made to cook food for his friends. "I've just thought of something. I can send up a smoke signal. If Bow Backus at the ranch sees it he will know it means we're here, and in trouble."

"How can you make a smoke signal?" asked Alice.

"Well, you use wet wood, to make a black smoke, and then you hold a blanket over the fire a moment. When you take it away up goes a single puff of smoke. Then you swing the blanket over the fire again, and cut off the smoke. In that way you can make a number of separate puffs.

"Bow and I have a signal code. If I can only get him to see this we'll be all right."

"It's worth trying," said Paul.

That day the Indians went at their ceremonies harder than ever. They were in a perfect frenzy, but the vigilance of the guards never relaxed. There was no chance to escape.

Russ, having nothing better to do, got many fine moving pictures through the hole in the hut, and later the films made a great hit in New York. It was the first time these peculiar rites had ever been shown on the screen. In fact, few white men had witnessed them.

Baldy was waiting for a chance to send up his smoke signal, but it was not until afternoon that he got it. Then, most of the Indians having gone off to a distant part of the *mesa*, for some new ceremony, Baldy made a thick smudge and he and Paul, holding a blanket over it, sent up a number of "puff balls." Russ took pictures of the signalling.

"There! If Bow only sees that he'll come runnin'!" Baldy cried.

But the smoke signal was the cause of considerable trouble to our friends. Hardly had Paul and Baldy finished sending the message, which they could only hope was seen and read at Rocky Ranch, than some of the Indians came back. They had noted what had been done, and they were very angry.

With furious gestures they rushed on the prisoners and for a moment it looked as though there would be trouble. Baldy and Paul stood steadily, revolvers in hand. But there was no need to use them. Jumping Horse rushed up, and drove back his men. Then he said something angrily to Baldy.

"What is it?" asked Mr. DeVere.

"He says we shall be punished for making the smoke," was the answer. "I don't know whether they think it's a signal or not; but it seems to have been contrary to some of their ceremonies. We'll have to sit tight and watch."

Muttering angrily, Jumping Horse went back to join the other Indians, and they seemed to hold a conference regarding the prisoners. Nothing was done immediately, however, in the way of punishment, and a little later the ceremonies went on.

It was growing dusk, and the howling and yelling of the Indians punctuated their caperings about a blood-red post in the center of the sandy circle. Then, suddenly, there was a fusillade of pistol shots from the direction of the trail, and at the same time the unmistakable shouts of cowboys.

"They're here!" yelled Baldy, jumping to his feet and firing his own revolver in the air. "To the rescue, boys! Here we be!"

CHAPTER XVIII

A RUSH OF STEERS

Russ came bounding from his hut, carrying with him the moving picture camera, its three legs trailing behind him.

"Come on, girls!" he cried, as he saw Ruth and Alice peering from their shelter. "It's all right!"

"Oh, what does it mean?" asked Ruth. "Where's daddy?"

"Here I am," answered Mr. DeVere.

"It's all right!" yelled Baldy, capering about, and vainly clicking his revolvers, for he had fired all the cartridges in the cylinders. "It's the boys from Rocky Ranch! They saw my signal and came to the rescue!"

"That you, Baldy?" shouted a voice out of the cloud of powder smoke that hid, for a moment, the cowboys from view.

"That's who it is, Bow!" was the answer. "Could you read my smoke?"

"I sure could, and we come a-runnin'. Are the girls safe?"

"Everybody's safe. But look out for yourself, these Indians are sort of riled at us."

From the group of Indians who had left their ceremonies, to rush toward the huts of their erstwhile captives at the sound of the shots and cheers, came deep-voiced mutterings. They were gathered in a group around their chief, Jumping Horse.

"Look out for 'em!" yelled Baldy.

"Don't worry," advised Pete Batso. "They haven't any weapons."

"Just my luck," groaned Russ, setting up his camera.

"What's the matter?" asked Alice, who now felt no alarm.

"Too dark to get a picture, and I had a little bit of film left on a reel. I might have got a dandy rescue scene; but now it's all up. Too bad!"

"Never mind, you got some good ones," Ruth comforted him.

"Yes, but that would have completed the picture—'Captured By the Indians.' However, it can't be helped. Maybe after all this excitement is over we can get the Indians to pose for us. I'll tell Mr. Pertell about it."

The rescuing cowboys had drawn rein in front of the lined-up Indians, near the huts of the captives. There was a goodly squad of cow punchers, and they seemed delighted to have been of some service to the picture players. Some of them were reloading their big revolvers, for they, like Baldy, in the excess of their spirits, had fired off every chamber. But no one had been hurt, for they merely shot in the air.

"Well, you got here, boys, I see," remarked Baldy.

"That's what we did!" cried Necktie Harry, who was flecking some dust off the end of his gaudy scarf.

"We saw your smoke talk about an hour ago," explained Bow. "First I was sort of puzzled over it. I thought maybe it was the Indians, for I calculate it was about time for them to be at their high jinks.

"Then I caught the private signal you and me made up, and I says: 'By Heck! Baldy's in trouble! Wasn't that what I said, Pete?" and he appealed to the foreman.

"That's what it was, Bow. Them's the very words you used. Says you: 'Baldy's in trouble,' says you. And then we come on the run."

"And we calculated we'd find the young ladies, and the rest of the outfit here, too," went on Bow. "When they didn't come back to the ranch last night we was all alarmed, and went off to the place they were goin' to make pictures. But there wasn't a sign of any trail there, and we didn't know what to think. We never dreamed you'd be on the *mesa*," he added to Mr. DeVere.

"I suppose we never should have come," admitted the actor. "It was on a sudden impulse, and sorry enough we were for it, too."

"Oh, but it all came out right," said Alice, trying to make herself look a little more presentable, for a night and more than a day spent as a prisoner in a little hut was not conducive to neatness of attire.

"And Russ got some fine pictures of the ceremonies,"

added Ruth.

"That's good!" cried Pete Batso. "When we started for here your manager said he reckoned his operator would have made good use of his time."

"We didn't know just what shape you was in," said Buster Jones, "only Baldy's message didn't say any of you was killed, so we hoped for the best."

"Yes, it might have been worse," agreed Baldy. "Well, now, let's travel. Did you have any trouble gettin' past their guard line, boys?" he asked.

"Nary a trouble," replied Pete. "We just rushed through before they knew what was up."

The captives were soon in the saddle again, and escorted by the cowboys made for the trail down to the plain. There were more angry mutterings from the Indians, but they made no effort to stop the retreat. Perhaps they realized it would be useless.

It was no easy matter descending the steep trail, but it was accomplished without mishap, and finally Rocky Ranch was reached. And it is needless to say that the captives were made welcome.

A little later, in clean garments, and after a good meal, they told of their adventures. The girls were quite the heroines of the hour, and held the center of the stage, rather to the discomfiture of Miss Pennington and Miss Dixon, who were in the habit of attracting all the attention they could.

"There's one picture I want very much to get," said Mr. Pertell, as he sat with his players in the living room of their quarters one evening.

"Name it," declared Mr. Norton, the owner, "and, if it's possible, I'll see that you get it."

"A cattle stampede," was the answer. "I want to show the steers in a mad rush, and the cowboys trying to stop them. But I don't suppose you can tell when one is going to happen."

"No, you can't tell when a real one is about to take place," the owner admitted, "but maybe we could fix up one for you."

"How do you mean?"

"Why, I mean we could take a bunch of steers, start them to running, and then the boys could come out and try to get them milling—that is, going around in a circle. That stops a stampede, usually. We could do that for you."

"And will you?" asked the manager, eagerly.

"Why, yes, if you want it. I'll speak to Pete Batso. He's had more experience than I have. We'll get up a stampede for you."

The cowboys entered into the spirit of the affair once it was mentioned to them, and arrangements were at once made.

As there might be some little danger of a refractory steer breaking loose and injuring someone, the ladies of the company only took part in the preliminary scenes.

These included the beginning of the drama in which the stampede was to play a principal part. It involved a little love story, and the lover, Paul, was afterward to be in peril through the cattle stampede.

The first part went off all right, Ruth and Alice acquitting themselves well in their characterizations. Their riding had improved very much, and they were sure of themselves in the saddle.

"Now, ladies," said Pete Batso, who was managing the cowboy end of the affair, "if you'll get over on that little mound you can see all that goes on and you won't be in any danger. We're goin' to stampede the cattle now!"

"Whoop-ee!" yelled the cowboys, as they rushed up at the signal, when Ruth and Alice, with Miss Pennington and Miss Dixon, had gone off some little distance.

"Get ready, Russ!" called Mr. Pertell.

"All ready," answered the young operator, as he took his place with his camera focused.

The steers, startled by the shots and shouts of the cowboys, began a mad rush.

"There's your stampede!" called Mr. Norton to Mr. Pertell. "Is that realistic enough for you?"

"Quite so, and thank you very much."

More and more wild became the rushing steers, as the cowboys drove them along in order that pictures might be made of them.

CHAPTER XIX

TOO MUCH REALISM

The shouting of the cowboys, the rushing of their intelligent ponies here—there—everywhere, seemingly—the fusillade of pistol shots, the thunder and bellowings of the steers and the thud of the ponies hoofs—all combined to make the scene a lively one.

The imitation stampede seemed to be a great success, and no one, not in the secret, could have told that it was not a real one.

"Over this way, Paul!" cried Baldy, who was taking part with the young actor. "I'm supposed to rescue you, and I can't do it if you keep so far away."

"But isn't it dangerous to ride so close to the steers?" asked Paul, who, while willing to do almost anything in the line of moving picture work, did not want to take needless chances.

"There's no danger as long as you're mounted," replied the cowboy, "and you've got a good horse under you. Come on!"

Accordingly Paul rode closer in, and the camera showed him in imminent danger of being trampled under the feet of the rushing steers.

But Baldy, who had done the same thing so often that he did not need to rehearse it, rode swiftly in and managed to "cut out" Paul, so that the actor was in no real danger. The cattle nearest to him were forced to one side.

Then, as called for in the action of the little drama, Mr. Switzer, who was a good horseman, having been in the German cavalry, rushed up to attack Paul. Of course it was but a pretended attack; but it looked real enough in the pictures.

Ruth and Alice, with the other spectators on the little mound, looked on with intense interest.

"Oh, I just wish I was on my pony!" cried Alice, as she looked at the scene of action.

"Alice, you do not!" protested Ruth.

"Yes, I do! Oh, it must be great to drive those cattle around that way!"

"You have a queer idea of fun," remarked Miss Pennington in a supercilious tone, as she looked in the small mirror of her vanity box to see what effect the sun and dust were having on her brilliant complexion. For it was dusty, with the thousands of hoofs tearing up the earth.

The main part of the action over, the cattle were now being "milled" by the cowboys. That is, the onward rush was being checked, and the steers were being made to go around in a circle.

Thus are stampedes, when real, gradually brought to an end.

"Well, it's all over," said Mr. Norton, as he stood beside the manager. "Is that about what you wanted?"

"Indeed it is. This film will sure make a hit. Those rivals of ours, who started out to take advantage of my plans and work, will be sadly left."

"You haven't seen any more of them?"

"Not since that fellow disappeared from here. He took himself and his camera off. I guess he weakened at the last moment."

"I had no idea he was a moving picture operator," said the ranch owner, "or I would never have hired him."

"Well, I guess no harm was done," Mr. Pertell rejoined.

The rush of the steers was gradually coming to a close when Mr. Norton, looking over to the far edge of the bunch of cattle, uttered a sudden cry of alarm.

"What's the matter?" asked Mr. Pertell, anxiously.

"Why, they seem to have started up all over again," was the reply. "You didn't tell them to put in a second scene of the stampede; did you?"

"No, indeed. We don't need it. Besides, Russ can't have any film left for this reel. He used up the thousand-foot, I'm sure, and he hasn't an extra one with him. What does it mean?"

"That's what I'd like to know. Those steers are certainly on the rush again, though. Hi, Baldy!" he called to the cowboy. "What are you starting 'em up again for?"

"Startin' who up?"

"The steers! Look at 'em!"

"Say, they *are* on the run again," agreed the bald-headed cowboy, who had ridden up to where Mr. Pertell and Mr. Norton stood. "Something must be wrong," and he set off on the gallop once more.

Meanwhile the steers, which had almost come to a rest, were again in motion. But they were not safely going about in a circle. Instead, they had started off in a long line and now were swinging around in a big circle and heading directly for the mound on which the young ladies were still standing.

Ruth and Alice had started down as they saw the cattle growing quiet, but now several of the cowboys shouted to them:

"Go back! Go back! This is a stampede in earnest."

"A stampede in earnest!" repeated Mr. Norton. "I wonder what started that?"

With a sudden rush the whole bunch of cattle were in motion, and headed in a solid mass for the mound.

"If they rush over that—" said Mr. Pertell in fear.

"This is too much realism!" cried Mr. Norton, putting spurs to his steed and racing off to help the cowboys. The latter had seen the danger of the girls, and were hastening to once more stop the stampede that had unexpectedly become a real one.

"Look at those fellows over there!" shouted Pete Batso as he rode up, his horse in a lather. "They're none of our crowd!" and he pointed to a group of horsemen who were riding away from the stampeded cattle instead of toward them.

"Who are they?" asked Mr. Pertell.

"I don't know, but they're a lot of cowards to run away, when we'll need all the help we can get to stem this rush!"

CHAPTER XX

IN THE OPEN

Thundering over the ground, the frightened cattle rushed on. After them came the cowboys, determined, at whatever cost, to turn the steers away from the little hill on which stood the four girls, clinging together, and in fear of their lives. For certainly it would be the end of life to fall beneath the hoofs of those on-rushing beasts.

"I can't understand what happened!" exclaimed Mr. Norton, as he rode on. "Those steers had all quieted down, when all of a sudden they started up again. Something must have happened."

He glanced over toward the mound. The cattle were still headed toward it. Would the cowboys be able to turn them aside in time?

"Head 'em off!"

"Shoot at 'em!"

"Head 'em away from that mound!"

Thus cried the cowboys as they raced to the rescue. They

Laura Lee Hope

were at rather a disadvantage, for their horses were winded and exhausted from the previous rushes to stop the pretended stampede, and now, when all their energies were needed to end a real one, the animals were not equal to the demand.

"Do you think they can stop 'em?" asked Russ of a passing cowboy. The young operator was still at his camera, but he was not going to take any pictures if Ruth, Alice and the others were really in danger.

"Of course we'll stop 'em!" cried the cowboy, with supreme confidence in his ability and that of his companions.

"Then I might as well get a film of this," decided Russ. "It would be a pity to let a real stampede get away from me. I can cut out some of the other pictures."

He ran to where he had left a spare camera and soon was grinding away at the handle, making views of a real and dangerous stampede.

"Oh, what shall we do?" gasped Alice, as she clung to her sister on the mound of safety.

"We can't do anything," answered Alice, solemnly—"except to wait. They may divide and pass to either side of us. I've read of such things happening."

"Oh, if they come any nearer I'll faint—I know I shall!" murmured Miss Dixon.

"That's the surest way to be trampled on," remarked Alice, calmly. "Just faint, and fall down and—"

She paused significantly.

"I sha'n't do anything of the kind!" cried the other actress with more spirit. "I won't do it just because you want me to! There!"

It was a silly thing to say, but then, she was half-hysterical. In fact, all four were.

"That's what I wanted to do—rouse her up," observed Alice to her sister. "It's our only safety—to remain upright. And we might try to frighten the cattle."

"How?" asked Ruth.

"Let's shout and yell—and wave things at them. We've got parasols. Let's wave them—open and shut them quickly. That will make flashes of color, and it may frighten the steers. Come on, girls—it's worth trying!"

The others fell in with her plan at once, and the spectacle was presented of four young ladies, perched on a hill, toward which a thousand or more steers were rushing, waving their parasols, opening and shutting them and yelling at the top of their voices.

"Are—are they stopping any?" asked Miss Pennington, anxiously.

"I—I'm afraid not," faltered Alice.

And then, just in the nick of time, there came riding around one side of the stampeding cattle a group of the Rocky Ranch cowboys. They had succeeded in reaching the head of the bunch of steers, and now had a chance to turn the excited cattle to one side—to mill them again.

"Hi—yi!" yelled the cowboys.

"Hi—yi!"

Bang! Bang! boomed the revolvers.

"Shoot right in their faces!" cried Buster Jones, as he fired point blank at the steers.

Most of the cowboys had blank cartridges in their pistols for the purpose of making a noise. But others had real bullets, and with these some of the wildest of the steers were killed. It was absolutely necessary to do this to stop the rush.

And this was just what was needed, for the fallen cattle tripped up others and soon there was a mound of the living bodies on the ground, offering an effectual barrier to those behind.

The cattle were now almost at the hill where the four young ladies stood in fear and trembling, but with the advent of the cowboys new hope had come to them.

"Now we're all right!" cried Alice, joyfully.

"How do you know?" Miss Pennington wanted to know.

"You'll see. They'll stop the stampede," was the confident answer.

And this was done. With the piling up of some of the steers into an almost inextricable mass, and the dividing of the other bunch just as they reached the foot of the mound, the danger to the girls was over.

In two streams of living animals the steers passed on either side of the little hill, and after running a short distance farther they came to a halt, being taken in charge by other cowboys who rode up from the rear on fresh horses.

Other horses were brought up for the girls to ride, as they were too weak and "trembly" to walk. Besides, it is always safer to be in the saddle among the lot of Western steers.

"Oh, what a narrow escape!" panted Miss Dixon.

"It was," agreed Alice. "But it shows you what cowboys can do! It was just splendid!" she cried to Baldy Johnson, who was riding beside her.

"Glad you liked it, Miss," he responded, breathing hard, "but it was rather hot work all around."

"You're not hurt; are you, girls?" cried Mr. DeVere as he came up to them, having had no part in the drama, but having heard in the ranch house of the real stampede.

"Not a bit, Daddy!" answered Alice. "I don't believe the steers would have trampled us anyhow."

"Well," remarked Baldy, slowly. "I don't want to scare you; but for a minute there I thought it was all up with you—I did for a fact."

"Some stampede!" cried Paul, as he rode up, looking almost like a cowboy himself.

"And some film!" laughed Russ, delighted that he had gotten one of the real stampede, now that his friends were out of danger.

"But I can't understand it," said Mr. Norton. "What started the cattle off the second time? They were really frightened at something."

"Did you see those men over that way?" asked the ranch owner, pointing in the direction where he had observed the retreating cowboy band.

"I saw 'em," admitted Pete, "but I thought they were some of our boys that you'd sent up to the North pasture."

"They weren't from Rocky Ranch!" declared the owner of the Circle Dot outfit.

"Well, if they were strange punchers, maybe they frightened our steers," suggested Baldy.

"They might have," admitted Mr. Norton. "But I was thinking that perhaps they were rustlers, trying to ride off a bunch, and they became frightened when they saw us all on hand."

"It might be," admitted Pete Batso. "I'll have a look around after we get the critters in the corral."

Ruth and Alice, as well as Miss Pennington and Miss Dixon, were so nervous and upset that it was thought advisable not to attempt any more pictures that day.

Most of the members of the Comet Film Company sat about the ranch house, talking over recent events, or studying parts for new plays. Some of the cowboys went off on the trail, trying to find traces of the strange men, but they returned unsuccessful.

The next days were spent in getting simple scenes about Rocky Ranch, no very hard work being done. These scenes would afterward be interspersed with more elaborate ones.

When moving picture films are made, it is usual to

photograph all the scenes of one kind first, whether or not they come in sequence. Thus, if one scene shows action taking place in a parlor, and the next scene calls for something going on out on the lawn, and the third scene is aboard a steamboat, while the fourth one is back in the parlor, the two parlor scenes will be taken one after the other, on the same film, at the same time, regardless of the fact that something came in between. Later on the outdoor scenes will be made, all at once. Then, when the film is developed and printed it is cut and fastened together to show the scenes in the order called for in the scenario.

Thus it was planned to make all the simple scenes around the ranch house first, and later to film a number of more important ones out in the open.

"We're going to rough it for a while," announced Mr. Pertell to his company one evening.

"Rough it!" cried Miss Pennington. "Have we done anything else since we left New York, pray?"

"Well, we're going to rough it more roughly then," went on the manager, with a smile. "I am going to have a series of films showing the life of the cowboys when off on the round-up. I want some of you in the scenes also, so I shall take most of you along.

"We will go into the open, and live out of doors. We will take along a 'grub wagon,' and other wagons for sleeping quarters for the ladies. There will be as many comforts as is possible to take, but I am sure you will all enjoy it so much you will not mind the discomfort. We will sleep out under the stars, and it will do you all good."

"I'm sure it's doing me good out here," said Mr. DeVere.

"My throat is much better."

"Glad to hear it," the manager responded. "Yes, we will live out of doors for perhaps a week—camping, so to speak; but on the move most of the time. And that will bring our stay at Rocky Ranch to a close. But there will be plenty to do before then," he added quickly, as he saw the look of disappointment on the face of Alice.

"Oh, I like it too much here to leave," she said. In fact Alice seemed to like every place. She could make herself at home anywhere.

Plans were made the next day, and nearly all the members of the company, save Mrs. Maguire and the two children, were to go on the trip across the prairies.

Big wagons, of the old-fashioned "prairie schooner" type, were made ready. In these the ladies would live when they were not in the saddle. There was also a "grub" wagon, in which food would be carried. It contained a small stove so that better meals could be prepared than would be possible over a campfire.

Then with plenty of spare horses, and with the camera and a good supply of film, the moving picture company and several cowboys set off one morning over the rolling plains.

Many scenes were filmed, some of them most excellent. It was not all easy going, for often there would be failures and the work would have to be done all over again. But no one grumbled, and really the life was a happy one. Even Mr. Sneed seemed to enjoy himself, and the former vaudeville actresses condescended to say it was "interesting."

One day an important film had been made and the work

involved was so hard that everyone was glad to go to their "bunks" early. Mr. Pertell, Russ and Mr. DeVere occupied a large tent near the wagons where the ladies had their quarters.

There was some little disturbance during the night, caused by one of the dogs barking, but the cowboys who roused to look about could find nothing wrong. But in the morning when Russ went to prepare his camera for that day's work he uttered an exclamation of dismay.

"What's the matter?" asked Mr. Pertell.

"That big reel I took yesterday, and which I put in the light-tight box for safe keeping, is gone!" cried the young operator.

CHAPTER XXI

THE BURNING GRASS

The announcement made by Russ caused considerable surprise, and, on the part of Mr. Pertell, dismay.

"You don't mean that big reel—that important one which is a sort of key to all the rest—is missing; do you?" he asked.

"That's it," replied Russ, ruefully. "It's clean gone!"

"Maybe you didn't look carefully, or perhaps you put it in some other place than you thought."

"I'm not in the habit of doing that with undeveloped film," replied the young operator. "If it was a reel ready for the projector I might mislay it, for I'd know the light couldn't harm it. But undeveloped reels, that the least glint of light would spoil—I take precious good care of them, let me tell you. And this one is gone."

"Let's have another look," suggested Mr. Pertell, hopefully.

He went into the tent from which Russ had just emerged, and the latter showed him where he had placed the reel. It was enclosed in its own case as it came from the camera, and that case, as an additional protection, was placed in a light-tight black box. This box would hold several reels; but that night only one, and the most important of those taken on the trip, was put in it.

"Look!" suddenly exclaimed Mr. DeVere, who had followed the two into the tent. "That's how your reel was taken!" and he pointed to a slit in the wall of the tent, close to where the black box had stood. So clean was the cut, having evidently been made with a very sharp instrument, that only when the wind swayed the canvas was it noticeable.

"By Jove! You're right!" cried Mr. Pertell. "That's how they got it, Russ. Someone sneaked up outside the tent, slit it open, reached in and lifted out the reel. It was done when we were asleep and—"

"That's what made the dogs bark!" exclaimed Russ. "Now the question is: Who was it?"

He looked at Mr. Pertell as he spoke, and at once a light of understanding came into the eyes of the manager.

"You mean—?" the latter began.

"Those fellows from the International!" finished Russ, quickly. "They must be still on our trail."

"What's the trouble?" asked Baldy Johnson, from outside the tent. "Has anything happened?"

"Oh, don't say there's more trouble," chimed in Ruth, as she came down out of the wagon where she and Alice slept. "What has happened now?"

"Nothing much, except that we've been robbed," spoke Russ,

ruefully. "Our big reel is gone." To the cowboys and others of the company who crowded up he showed the slit in the tent wall, through which the theft had been perpetrated.

"Hum! I guess those fellows were smarter than we were," replied Baldy. "We scurried around in the night, but they gave us the slip."

"And we didn't see a sign of 'em, neither!" added Buster Jones.

"Say, fellows, if this ever gets back to Rocky Ranch," went on Necktie Harry, as he adjusted a flaming red scarf, "we'll never hear the last of it. To think we heard a racket, got up, and let something be taken right from under our noses and didn't see it done—Good-night! as the poet says."

"Boys, we've got to make good!" declared Bow Backus. "We've got to take the trail after these scamps, and get back them pictures. It's up to us!"

"Whoop-ee! That's what it is!" shouted Necktie Harry, firing his gun.

"Oh, isn't this fine!" cried Alice, as she joined Ruth. "There will be a real chase and—"

"Oh, how can you like such things?" asked Ruth. "It may be something terrible!"

"Pooh! I don't see how it can be. If they have something that belongs to us we have a right to get it back," and Alice shook back the hair that was falling over her shoulders, for she was to take part in several pictures that day as a "cowgirl," and was dressed in a picturesque, if not exactly correct, costume, with short skirt, leggins and all.

"Oh, I hope there won't be any—bloodshed!" faltered Miss Pennington.

"They'll probably only use their lassoes," replied Alice, with a smile. "Oh dear! I hope breakfast will soon be ready. I'm as hungry as a—"

"Alice!" warned Ruth, with a gentle look. She was still trying to correct her sister's habit of slang.

"As hungry as if I hadn't eaten since last night," finished Alice with a mocking laugh. "There, sister mine!" and she blew her a kiss from the tips of her rosy fingers.

"Well, it's easy enough to say: 'Get after the fellows who took the reel,'" spoke Baldy Johnson, "but who were they, and where shall we start?"

"It must have been someone who knew where we kept the reels in the light-tight box," said Russ. "Otherwise he would have cut several places in the tent to reach in and feel around. And there is only one cut. So it must have been somebody who knew about this tent."

"Regular detective work, that," remarked Necktie Harry, quickly, looking admiringly at Russ.

"Say! I have it!" cried Baldy Johnson. "Those fellows who rode in yesterday to watch us work. It was one of them."

"You mean the boys from the Double ranch?" asked Buster.

"Them's the ones," answered Baldy. Just before the close of the making pictures the day before a crowd of cowboys from a nearby cattle range had ridden up, and looked on interestedly. They were returning from a round-up. Some of them were known to the boys from Rocky Ranch, and there had been an exchange of courtesies.

"'Them's the guilty parties,' as the actor folks say," sung out Bow Backus.

"I think you are right," agreed Mr. Pertell.

"But I can't see what object cowboys would have in taking a film—and an undeveloped one at that," said Russ. "I can't believe it."

"Maybe the International firm bribed them, or maybe one of their men was disguised as a cowboy," suggested Mr. DeVere.

"That's possible," admitted Russ.

"Well, we'll soon find out," declared Baldy. "Come on, boys. Grub up and then we'll ride over."

The visit to Double X ranch proved fruitless, however, except in one particular. The cowboys attached to that "outfit" easily proved that they had not been near the camp of the picture makers.

"But there was one fellow who rode with us," said the foreman. "He was a stranger to us. Looked to be a cow-puncher, and *said* he was, from down New Mexico way. He was with us when we were at your place, and when we rode away he branched off. It might have been him."

"I'm sure it was," declared Mr. Pertell. "Now, how can we get hold of him?"

But that was a question no one could answer, and though

several of the cowboys took the trail after the stranger, he was not to be found. The missing film seemed to have disappeared for good.

It was a great loss, but there was no help for it, and plans were made to go through the big scene again, though not until later.

"I have something else I want filmed now," said Mr. Pertell. "We will make that 'lost' scene we spoke of last night and then try a novelty."

"Something new?" asked Mr. Bunn. "I hope I don't have to be lassoed again," for that had been his most recent "stunt."

"No, we'll let you off easy this time," laughed Mr. Pertell. "All you'll have to do will be to escape from a prairie fire."

"A prairie fire!" gasped the Shakespearean actor. "I refuse to take that chance."

"Don't worry," said the manager. "It will only be a small, imitation blaze. I want to get some scenes of that," he went on to explain to the cowboys. "In the early days of the West prairie fires were one of the terrible features. I realize that now, of course, with the West so much more built up, they are not so common. But I think we could arrange for a small one, and burn the grass over a limited area. It would look big in a picture."

"Yes, it could be done," admitted Baldy. "We'll help you."

Two or three more days were spent in the open, traveling over the prairie, making various films. Then a suitable location for the "prairie fire" was found and a little rehearsal held.

"That will do very well," said Mr. Pertell at the conclusion. "We'll film the scene to-morrow."

The arrangements were carefully made, and in a big open place the tall dry grass was set on fire. The flames crackled, and great clouds of black smoke rolled upward.

"Go ahead now, Russ!" called the manager. "That ought to make a fine film! Come on, you people—Mr. DeVere, Ruth, Alice—get in the picture. Register fear!"

CHAPTER XXII

HEMMED IN

Elaborate preparations had been made for this prairie fire picture. In fact, in a way, the whole story of the drama "East and West" hinged on this scene. It was the climax, so to speak—the "big act" if the play had been on the real stage. Naturally Mr. Pertell was anxious to have everything right.

And so it seemed to be going. The flames crackled menacingly, and the black smoke rolled up in great clouds that would show well on the film.

In brief, this action of the play was to depict the hardships of one of the early Western settlers. He had taken up a section of land, built himself a rude house, and was living there with his family when the prairie fire came, and he was forced to flee.

Of course all this was "only make believe," as children say. But it was put on for the film in a very realistic manner. Pop Snooks had constructed a slab house, with the aid of the cowboys, who said it was as near the "real thing" as possible. Later on the house, which was but a shell, and intended only for the "movies," would be destroyed by fire.

Scenes would be shown in which the settler (Mr. DeVere) and his helpers would try to extinguish the fire before they fled from it.

The first scene showed the fire starting, with the plowmen (Mr. Bunn and Mr. Sneed) in the fields at work. They were seen to stop, to shade their eyes with their hands and look off toward the distant horizon, where a haze of smoke could be seen. The big distances which were available on the prairies of the West, made this particularly effective in a film picture.

The taking of the film had so far advanced that the warning had come to those in the slab shanty. There were gathered Ruth, Alice, Miss Pennington, Miss Dixon, Paul and others.

"Ride! Ride for your lives!" cried Mr. Sneed, dashing up on one of the plow horses. "The prairies are on fire and it's coming this way lickity-split!"

Of course his words would not be heard by the moving picture audiences, though those accustomed to it can read the lip motions. Really the words need not have been said, and it was this feature of the "movies" that enabled Mr. DeVere to take up the work when he had failed in the "legitimate" because of his throat ailment.

"Flee for your lives!" cried Mr. Sneed. "We're going to try to burn it back, or plow a strip that it can't get over."

Thereupon ensued a scene of fear and excitement at the slab hut. A wagon was hastily brought up by some of the cowboys, who were taking part in the picture, and the household goods, (provided of course by the ever-faithful Pop Snooks), were hastily packed into it.

Then the girls and others, with every sign of fear and dismay, properly "registered" for the benefit of those who would later see the film in the darkened theaters, gathered together their personal belongings, and entered the wagon.

Meanwhile Russ was kept busy getting different views of the big scene. Sometimes there would be shown the raging fire sweeping onward, the black clouds of smoke rolling upward, and the red tongues of flame leaping out. In reality the fire was only a small one, but by cleverly manipulating the camera, and taking close views, it was made to appear as if it was a raging conflagration.

As Russ would have difficulty in showing alternate views of the fire itself and the preparations at the slab hut to flee from it, Mr. Pertell, at times, worked an extra camera himself. Thus the time was shortened, for the fire was something that could not be held back, as could something of purely human agency.

"Ride! Ride for your lives!" now shouted Mr. Sneed, as he sat on his heaving horse, ready to ride back and help fight the fire. With dramatic gestures he pointed ahead, seemingly to a place of safety. "Ride for your lives!"

"But you? What of you?" cried Miss Pennington, as she held out her hands to him imploringly. She was supposed (in the play) to be in love with him.

"I go back—to do my duty!" he replied, as his lines called for.

There was a dramatic little scene and then Miss Pennington, "registering" weeping, went inside the "prairie schooner," as the big covered wagon was called.

Paul, on the driver's seat, cracked his whip at the horses and

Laura Lee Hope

the vehicle lumbered off, Ruth, Alice and the others who were inside, looking back as if with regret at the home that was soon to be destroyed.

Mr. Sneed remained for a moment, posing on the back of his horse, and then, with a farewell wave of his hand he rode back to join Mr. Bunn and the others in fighting the fire that had been "made to order." Mr. DeVere, too, after seeing his family off in the wagon, leaped on a horse and also galloped back to help fight the flames. There had been a dramatic parting between him and his daughters—for the purposes of the film, of course.

"Say, this fire's gettin' a little hot!" cried Baldy, who, with the other cowboys, had been detailed to put out the blaze. Mr. Pertell was there to get a film of them, while Russ, a considerable distance away, was to film the on-rushing wagon containing those fleeing from the blaze. The picture was so arranged as to show alternately views of the wagon and the fire fighters. Always, however, there was the background of the black smoke when the wagon was shown tearing over the prairie, and the smoke constantly grew blacker.

"Get at it now, boys!" cried the manager, grinding away at the handle of his camera. "Put in some lively work! Mr. Sneed, don't be afraid of the fire. You're standing off too far."

The plot of the play was that first an attempt would be made to beat out the fire, by means of bundles of wet brush dipped in a nearby brook. This plan was to fail, and then an attempt would be made to "fight fire with fire." That is, the prairie grass would be set ablaze some distance ahead of the line of fire, and allowed to burn toward it. This would make a blackened strip, bare of fuel for the flames, and the hope was—or it used to be when prairie fires in the West were common—that this would check the advancing blaze.

For a few seconds the men fought frantically to beat out the fire, then Mr. DeVere exclaimed, with a dramatic gesture:

"It is no use! We must fight fire with fire!"

The men ran back some distance, Mr. Pertell taking his camera back the same space. Then the prairie was set ablaze in a number of places, at points nearer the slab cabin which was, as yet, untouched.

The scene of starting a counter-fire was a short one, for it was quickly discovered, in reality as well as in the play, as planned, that the wind was in the wrong direction. It simply advanced the flames nearer the cabin.

"It's of no use, boys!" cried Mr. DeVere. "We must plow a bare strip."

"Bring up the horses and plows!" ordered Baldy. A number of these had been held in reserve, out of sight of the camera, and they now came up on the rush. The idea was that neighboring settlers, having sighted the prairie fire, had come to the aid of their friends in the slab cabin.

Horses were quickly hitched to the plows, and the work of making a number of furrows of damp earth, to act as a barrier to the flames, was started.

While Mr. Pertell was filming this, Russ was busy getting views of the on-rushing wagon containing the refugees. Several times the team was stopped to enable the operator to go on ahead, and show it coming across the prairie. This gave a different background each time.

It was after one of these halts, and just when the team was started up again that Alice, who was on the front seat with Paul, the driver, cried out:

"See! There is smoke and fire ahead of us, too! What does it mean?"

For an instant they were all startled, and then, as Ruth looked behind them, and saw the fiercer flames, and the blacker smoke there, she gasped:

"We are hemmed in! Hemmed in by the prairie fire!"

CHAPTER XXIII

THE ESCAPE

Paul pulled up the rushing horses with a jerk that set them back on their haunches. There were cries of alarm from the interior of the wagon, and from the front and rear peered out anxious faces.

"What is it? Oh, what is it?" cried Miss Dixon.

"There's a fire ahead of us," replied Alice, and her voice was calmer now. She realized that their situation might be desperate, and that there would be need of all the presence of mind each one possessed.

"A fire ahead of us!" repeated Miss Pennington. "Then let's turn back. Probably Mr. Pertell wanted this to happen. It's all in the play. I don't see anything to get excited about."

For once in her life she was more self-possessed than any of the others, but it was due to the bliss of ignorance.

"Let's turn back," she suggested. "That seems the most reasonable thing to do. And I wonder if you would mind if I rode on the seat next to your friend Paul," she went on to Alice. "I'd like to have the center of the stage just for once, as sort of a change," and her tone was a bit malicious.

"I'm sure you're welcome to sit here," responded Alice, quietly. "But, as for turning back, it is impossible. Look!" and she waved her hand toward the rear. There the black clouds of smoke were thicker and heavier, and the shooting flames went higher toward the heavens.

"Oh!" gasped Miss Pennington, and then she realized as she had not done before—the import of Ruth's words:

"We are hemmed in!"

"Can't—can't we go back?" gasped Miss Dixon.

"The fire behind us is worse than that before us," said Paul, in a low voice. "Perhaps, after all, we can make a rush for it."

"No, don't try dot!" spoke Mr. Switzer, and somehow, in this emergency, he seemed very calm and collected. "Der horses vould shy und balk at der flames," went on the German, who seemed far from being funny now. He was deadly in earnest. "Ve can not drive dem past der flames," he added.

"But what are we to do?" asked Paul. "We can't stay here to be—"

He did not finish the sentence, but they all knew what he meant.

"Vait vun minute," suggested the German. He stood up on the seat so as to bring his head above the canvas top of the wagon. Those in it, save Paul, who remained holding the reins to quiet the very restive horses, had jumped to the ground.

"The wind is driving on der flames dot are back of us," said Mr. Switzer in a low voice. "It is driving dem on."

He turned in the opposite direction, where the flames and smoke were less marked, but still dangerously in evidence.

"Und dere, too," the German murmured. "Der vind dere, too, is driving dem on—driving dem on! I don't understand it. Dere must be a vacuum caused by der two fires."

"Well, what's to be done?" asked Mr. Towne, who formed one of the fleeing party. "We can't stay here forever— between two fires, you know."

"Yah! I know," remarked Mr. Switzer, slowly. "Ve must get avay. We cannot go back, ve cannot go forvarts. Den ve must—"

"Oh, if we can't go back, what has become of those whom we left behind?" cried Ruth. "My father—and the others?"

Her tearful face was turned toward Alice.

"They—they may be all right," said the younger girl, but her voice was not very certain.

"The—the fire must be at the cabin by now," went on Ruth. "If—if anything has happened that they were not able to get the flames under control—"

She, too, did not finish her portentous sentence.

"Ve cannot go forvarts," murmured Mr. Switzer, "und ve cannot go back. Den de only oder t'ing to do iss to go to der left or right. Iss dot not so Paul, my boy?"

"It certainly is, and the sooner the better!" cried the young actor. "Get into the wagon again and I'll try the left. It looks more open there. And hurry, please, it's getting hard to hold the horses. They want to bolt."

There were four animals hitched to the wagon, and it was all Paul could do to manage them. Every moment they were getting more and more excited by the sight and smell of the smoke and flames.

Into the wagon piled the refugees, and Paul gave the horses their heads, guiding them over the prairie in a direction to the left, for the smoke seemed less thick there. It was a desperate chance, but one that had to be taken.

Ruth and Alice, going to the rear of the vehicle, looked out of the opening for a sight of their father and the others coming up on the gallop, possibly to report that the fire had gotten beyond their control.

But there was no sight of them.

"Oh, what can have happened?" murmured Ruth with clasped hands, while tears came into her eyes.

"Don't worry, dear," begged Alice.

"But I can't help it."

"Perhaps they are all right, Ruth. They may have gone to one side, just as we did, and of course they couldn't ride towards us until they got beyond the path of the flames."

"Oh, if I could only hope so!" the elder girl replied.

The wagon was rocking and swaying over the uneven ground

as the horses galloped on. Russ, who had run to one side when the halt was made, held up his hand as a signal to halt. He had taken films until the vehicle was too close to be in proper focus.

"Do get up and get in with us!" begged Ruth. "You must not stay here any longer."

"I was thinking that myself," he said grimly.

A glance back showed that the fire there had increased in intensity, and the one in front was also growing. There was presented the rather strange sight of two fires rushing together, though the one in the rear, or behind the refugees, came on with greater speed, urged by a stronger wind. As Mr. Switzer had said, a vacuum might have been created by the larger conflagration, which made a draft that blew the smaller fire toward the bigger one.

"Do you see any opening, either backward or forward?" asked Russ of Paul, when they had gone on for perhaps half a mile.

"Not yet," answered the driver. "Though the smoke, does seem to be getting a bit thinner ahead there, on the left."

But it was a false hope, and going on a little farther it was seen that the two fires had joined about a mile ahead, completely cutting off an advance in that direction.

It was as though our friends were in an ever narrowing circle of flame. There was a fire behind them, in front of them and to one side. There only remained the one other side.

Would there be an opening in the circle—an opening by which they could escape?

"Ve must go to der right," cried Mr. Switzer.

"Und I vill drive, Paul. I haf driven in der German army yet, und I know how."

They were now tearing along in a lane bordered with fire on either side, with raging flames behind them. Their only hope lay in front.

"Well, these films may never be developed," observed Russ, grimly, as took his camera off the tripod, "but I'm going to get a picture of this prairie fire. It's the best chance I've ever had—and it may be my last. But I'm not going to miss it!"

And so, as the wagon careened along between the two lines of fire, Russ took picture after picture, holding the camera on his knees.

On and on the frantic horses were driven, until finally Paul, who was on the seat beside Mr. Switzer, with Russ between them taking pictures, called out:

"Hold on! Wait a minute. I think I hear voices!"

The horses were held back, not without difficulty, and then as the noise of their galloping, and the sound of the creaking wagon ceased, there was heard the unmistakable shouts of cowboys, and the rapid firing of revolvers.

"There they are!" cried Alice.

"Oh, if daddy is only there!" Ruth replied.

"Go on!" cried Paul to the German, and again the horses were given their heads.

But now, even above the noise made by the wagon and the galloping steeds, could be heard the welcome shouts which told that some, at least, of those left behind were still alive. The girls were crying now, in very joy, though their anxiety was not wholly past.

On and on galloped the horses. And then Paul cried:

"There's a way! There's a way out! The fire hasn't burned around the whole circle yet."

He pointed ahead. Through the smoke clouds could be seen an open space of grass that was not yet burned, and beyond that sparkled the waters of a wide but shallow creek.

There was safety indeed! They had escaped the flames by a narrow margin.

And as the wagon rushed for this haven of refuge, there came sweeping up from one side a group of cowboys, urging their horses to top speed, while, in their midst was Mr. DeVere, Mr. Pertell and the others of the moving picture company who had been left to finish the scene at the slab cabin.

CHAPTER XXIV

A DISCLOSURE

"Into the creek! Drive right in!" cried Baldy Johnson. "Run the wagon right in! It's a good bottom and you can go all the way across!"

"Go on!" called Mr. Switzer to his horses, and the steeds, nothing loath, darted for the cooling water. Indeed it was very hot now, for the fire was close, and it was still coming on, in an ever-narrowing circle.

"Go ahead, boys! Into the creek with you! It's our last chance, and our only one!" went on Baldy. "Into the water with you!"

And into the welcome coolness of the creek splashed the cowboys on their ponies and the wagon containing the refugees.

"Where are you going?" cried Ruth, as Russ swung himself down off the seat.

"I'm going to get this last film, showing the escape," he answered. "It's too good a chance to miss."

"But you'll be burned!" she exclaimed. "The fire is coming closer."

And indeed the flames, closing up the circle of fire, were drawing nearer and nearer.

"I'll be all right," he assured her. "I just want to get some pictures showing the wagon and the cowboys going across the creek. Then I'll wade across myself. Of course I'd like to get a front view, but I'll have to be content with a rear one."

And as the wagon drawn by the frantic horses plunged into the water, followed by the shouting cowboys and the members of the film company, Russ calmly set his camera up on the edge of the stream, and took a magnificent film that afterward, under the title "The Escape from Fire," made a great sensation in New York.

The brave young operator remained until he felt the heat of the flames uncomfortably close and then, holding his precious camera high above his head, he waded into the creek. The waters did not come above his waist, and when he was safe on the other side with his friends, finding he had a few more feet of film left, he took the pictures showing the fire as it raged and burned the last of the grass, and other pictures giving views of the exhausted men, women and horses in a temporary camp.

"Whew! But that was hot work!" cried Mr. Bunn, mopping his face.

"You're right," agreed Mr. Pertell. "I don't believe I'll chance any more prairie fires. This one rather got away from us."

There was a shout from some of the cowboys who stood in a group on the bank of the creek.

"Look! Look at those fellows!" cried Bow Backus. "They just got out of the fire by a close shave—same as we did."

They all looked to where he pointed.

There, crossing the stream higher up, and seemingly at a place which the fire had only narrowly missed, were several horsemen. Their steeds appeared exhausted, as though they had had a hard race to escape.

"What outfit is that, fellows?" asked Baldy Johnson. "I don't know of any punchers attached to a ranch that's within this here fire range."

"There isn't any," declared Necktie Harry.

"But where did those cowboys come from?" persisted Baldy.

"They're not cowboys!" declared Necktie Harry, looking to see if his scarf had suffered any from the smoke and cinders. "Did you ever see real cow punchers ride the way they do—like sacks of meal. They're fakes, that's what they are!"

For an instant Baldy stared at the speaker, and then cried:

"That's it! I couldn't understand it before, but I do now. It's all clear!"

"What is?" asked Mr. Pertell, who was still, rather wrought up by the danger into which he had thrown his players.

"Why, about this blaze. I couldn't for the life of me understand how it was it could burn two ways at once. But now I do."

"You mean those fellows set another fire?" asked

Bow Backus.

"That's my plain identical meanin'," declared Baldy. "Them scoundrels started another fire after we did ours."

"Oh, how terrible!" exclaimed Ruth.

"Wait; hold on, Miss! I'm not goin' so far as to accuse 'em of doin' it purposely," the cowboy went on, earnestly. "They may not have meant it. The grass is pretty dry just now, and a little fire would burn a long way. It's jest possible they may have made a blaze to bile their coffee, and the wind carried sparks into a bunch of grass. But I have my suspicions."

"Why, who could they be, to do such a dastardly thing as that?" demanded Mr. DeVere.

"That's what I want to know," put in Mr. Pertell.

Baldy turned sharply to the manager.

"Who's been followin' on your trail ever since you started out to make your big drama 'East and West'?" he asked.

"Who—who!" repeated Mr. Pertell. "Why—why those sneaks from the International Picture Company—that's who."

"That's them," declared Baldy, laconically, as he pointed to the retreating horsemen. "That's them, and they're the fellows who sot this second fire that so nearly wrecked us."

"Is it possible!" ejaculated Mr. DeVere.

"I'm sure of it," declared Baldy. "I ain't got no real proof; but I've seen a good many fires in my day, and they don't start all by their ownselves—not two of 'em, anyhow. You can bank on them bein' your enemies, if you'll excuse my slang," he said in firm tones.

"Do you really mean it?" asked Mr. Pertell, in amazement.

"I sure do, friend. I'm not sayin' they started it to hurt any of you; but they wanted to spoil your picture, I'm sure of it."

There was a moment of silence, and then Bow Backus cried out in loud tones:

"Fellers, there's only one thing to do: Let's take after them scamps and get 'em with the goods! Let's prove that they did this mischief. Come on, boys! Our horses are fresh enough now."

The tired cow ponies, almost worn out after their race to escape with their masters from the on-rushing flames, had been allowed to rest and now they were ready for hard work again.

In an instant, half a score of the sturdy cowboys were in the saddle, whooping and yelling in sheer delight at the prospective chase.

"I've got to get in on this!" cried Russ. "Wait a minute until I film the start, fellows, and then I'll get on a horse and take my camera. I'll go with you, and get the finish of this, too."

A new roll of film was quickly slipped into the camera and Russ dashed on ahead to show the on-coming cowboys in their rush to overtake the suspected men.

Then the young operator jumped into the saddle of a steed that was ready and waiting for him, and galloped on with his friends to get, if possible, the finish of the affair.

"Oh, isn't it just splendid!" cried Alice, clapping her hands.

"But it makes me so nervous!" protested Ruth.

"I just love to be nervous—this way," declared Alice, with a joyous laugh.

Away flew the eager cowboys, and those left behind proceeded to let their nerves quiet down after the strenuous times they had just passed through. The cook had come up and he at once prepared a little meal.

On the other side of the wide creek the prairie fire burned itself out. The blaze crept in the dry grass down to the very edge of the water, where it went out with puffs of steam, and vicious hisses.

"Oh, but I'm glad we're not there," sighed Ruth as she looked across at the smoke-palled and blackened stretch.

"Yes, it was a narrow escape," said her father.

"What happened after we left?" asked Alice.

"The fire really got a little too much for us," said Mr. Pertell. "And, as I had pictures enough, we decided to leave. We let the cabin burn, as we had arranged, and then came riding on.

"But the flames were a little too quick for us, and we had to turn off to one side. That's why we didn't get up to you more quickly. We were really quite worried about you."

CHAPTER XXV

THE ROUND-UP

"What's the matter?"

"Couldn't you catch them?"

"Did they get away?"

All needless questions, evidently, yet they were anxiously asked, for all that, when the tired and disappointed cowboys, led by Baldy Johnson, returned after the chase. It was dusk, and the prairie fire was almost out. Only a faint glow showed where, here and there, a bunch of thick grass was still blazing.

"They gave us the slip," complained Baldy in discouraged tones. "Their horses were fresher than ours were. Probably they got out of the way of the fire sooner than we did."

"Did you get close enough to recognize them?" Mr. Pertell wanted to know.

"I didn't know any of 'em," asserted Baldy. "Not that I got any too close," he added, grimly. "They sure can ride, even if they don't have our style."

"I'm not sure," remarked Russ, as he put away the camera which he had had no chance to use after filming the start of the cowboys, "I'm not sure, but I think I recognized one of the fellows as the chap who was at Rocky Ranch when we arrived there."

"Then he has others with him," said Mr. Pertell.

"Evidently."

"And they will probably try to do us some more mischief," went on the manager. "We still have several important films to make, and if they try to steal our ideas and get the pictures we go to so much trouble to make we may as well give up."

"Don't you do it!" cried Baldy Johnson. "Don't you do it! We'll get after these fellows the first thing in the morning, and round 'em up good and proper."

"That's what we will!" cried his companion. "Whoop-ee for the round-up!"

"We'll pay 'em for startin' that fire," went on Baldy.

"Yes, and for stampedin' those cattle, too," added Buster Jones.

"Do you think they did that?" Mr. Pertell asked, quickly.

"I wouldn't be a bit surprised," declared Buster. "If they was mean enough to start a fire to spoil the picture they wouldn't stop at a little thing like stampedin' a bunch of cattle. I'm sure they done it."

"Then all the more reason for runnin' 'em out of the country!" decided Baldy. "We'll get on the trail early in the mornin', boys."

"We're with you!" cried the others.

The camp, which had been made on the side of the creek where refuge had been taken from the fire, was soon in order. The cook wagon and supplies had been sent far away from the scene of the blaze when it was started, and it had come up by a different trail. Soon with tents erected, and with the sleeping wagon for the ladies in readiness, quiet settled down over the scene.

Believing that it was more necessary to capture or drive out of that section the rivals who were endeavoring to get ahead of him, Mr. Pertell decided not to make any more films until after the chase. Preparations for this were soon under way, next morning, and, save for a small guard of cowboys left in camp, all the men riders went after the suspected ones. Mr. DeVere remained with his daughters. Of course Russ went along to make the pictures.

It was some time before the searchers got on the proper trail. They followed one or two false ones at first, but finally were set right, and then they rode furiously.

"There they are!" cried Baldy, who had taken the lead. This was after a hasty lunch. He pointed to a group of fleeing horsemen.

"After 'em!" yelled Bow Backus.

"They shan't get away this time!" cried Buster Jones.

And they did not. Ride as the fleeing ones might, they were no match for their pursuers, and after a short chase, which Russ was able to get on the film, the fugitives were surrounded.

"Surrender!" yelled the cowboys of Rocky Ranch as they rode down their rivals.

And the others were glad enough to pull up their jaded steeds, for they had ridden far and hard to escape. But fate was against them.

"So it's you; is it, Wilson!" exclaimed Mr. Pertell, as he recognized the spy who had been detected in the studio.

"And there's that other chap!" exclaimed Russ, as he saw the man who had so suddenly left Rocky Ranch. "Now if we could only get back that roll of stolen film we'd be all right."

The prisoners were searched and bound, and on Wilson were found papers incriminating him and his confederates in both the moves against our friends. Other actions to take advantage of Mr. Pertell had also been planned.

But, best of all, the headquarters of the gang was disclosed and there, among other things, was found the missing roll of film, with the seals unbroken, showing that it was not spoiled, but could be developed and printed. So, after all, there was no need of making the big scene over again. The surreptitious pictures of the oil well were also recovered and destroyed.

And then, after no very gentle treatment, the Rocky Ranch cowboys ran out of the country the men who had been trying to take advantage of Mr. Pertell's work for the benefit of the International company.

"That's the way!"

"Run 'em out!"

"Give 'em some more!"

To these startling shouts were Wilson's men driven away, and glad enough they were to go. What other films they had taken on the sly were destroyed, and their cameras were confiscated. In fact all their efforts came to naught. It was disclosed, later, that they had not intended to endanger our friends by starting the prairie fire; only to spoil their plans.

"And now for the grand finale!" cried Mr. Pertell a few days later, when the return had been made to Rocky Ranch. "This will be the last scene in the great drama 'East and West.' There's to be a cowboy festival, with all sorts of stunts in horsemanship and lariat throwing. You've got a lot of work ahead of you, Russ."

There were busy days at Rocky Ranch. Cowboys from neighboring places rode over to take part in the fun and frolic, and Russ got many fine films.

"Oh, I don't know when I've enjoyed anything so much as I have this life in the West," said Alice, when the last film had been taken.

"Nor I," added Ruth. "It has been just glorious."

"And I am so much better," declared Mr. DeVere. "I would scarcely know I had a sore throat now."

"Oh, I'm so glad, Daddy dear!" exclaimed Alice, as she put her arms around his neck.

"And now we're going back to New York, and have a good, long rest," went on Ruth. "I shall be sorry to get into the stuffy city again."

"I won't," declared Miss Pennington. "I'm just dying for a sight of dear old Broadway," and as if that gave her a thought she gently powdered her nose. Perhaps it needed it, for she was very much sunburned.

"Well, you're going back to New York all right, as far as that is concerned," said Mr. Pertell, who had overheard part of the talk. "But as for a rest—well, I suppose I'll have to give you a little one, before we start off again."

"Oh, have you more plans in prospect?" asked Alice.

"Indeed I have, my dear young lady. We're going in for water stuff next."

And those of you who desire to follow further the careers of Ruth, Alice and their friends, may do so by reading the next volume of this series, to be called, "The Moving Picture Girls at Sea; Or, A Pictured Shipwreck That Became Real."

"One more day at Rocky Ranch!" cried Alice, as she came out on the veranda one glorious morning. "Oh, but I don't want to leave it!"

"Neither do I!" cried Paul, coming around the corner of the house so unexpectedly that Alice was startled. "Suppose we go for a last ride?" he suggested.

And together they rode over the prairies, side by side toward the Golden West.

*　*　*　*　*

　　　　Laura Lee Hope

ABOUT THE AUTHOR

Laura Lee Hope is a pseudonym used by the Stratemeyer Syndicate for the Bobbsey Twins and several other series of children's novels. Actual writers taking up the pen of Laura Lee Hope include Howard and Lilian Garis, Elizabeth Ward, Harriet (Stratemeyer) Adams, and Nancy Axelrad.

Choose from Thousands of 1stWorldLibrary Classics By

A. M. Barnard
Ada Leverson
Adolphus William Ward
Aesop
Agatha Christie
Alexander Aaronsohn
Alexander Kielland
Alexandre Dumas
Alfred Gatty
Alfred Ollivant
Alice Duer Miller
Alice Turner Curtis
Alice Dunbar
Allen Chapman
Alleyne Ireland
Ambrose Bierce
Amelia E. Barr
Amory H. Bradford
Andrew Lang
Andrew McFarland Davis
Andy Adams
Angela Brazil
Anna Alice Chapin
Anna Sewell
Annie Besant
Annie Hamilton Donnell
Annie Payson Call
Annie Roe Carr
Annonaymous
Anton Chekhov
Archibald Lee Fletcher
Arnold Bennett
Arthur C. Benson
Arthur Conan Doyle
Arthur M. Winfield
Arthur Ransome
Arthur Schnitzler
Arthur Train
Atticus
B.H. Baden-Powell
B. M. Bower
B. C. Chatterjee
Baroness Emmuska Orczy
Baroness Orczy
Basil King
Bayard Taylor
Ben Macomber
Bertha Muzzy Bower
Bjornstjerne Bjornson

Booth Tarkington
Boyd Cable
Bram Stoker
C. Collodi
C. E. Orr
C. M. Ingleby
Carolyn Wells
Catherine Parr Traill
Charles A. Eastman
Charles Amory Beach
Charles Dickens
Charles Dudley Warner
Charles Farrar Browne
Charles Ives
Charles Kingsley
Charles Klein
Charles Hanson Towne
Charles Lathrop Pack
Charles Romyn Dake
Charles Whibley
Charles Willing Beale
Charlotte M. Braeme
Charlotte M. Yonge
Charlotte Perkins Stetson
Clair W. Hayes
Clarence Day Jr.
Clarence E. Mulford
Clemence Housman
Confucius
Coningsby Dawson
Cornelis DeWitt Wilcox
Cyril Burleigh
D. H. Lawrence
Daniel Defoe
David Garnett
Dinah Craik
Don Carlos Janes
Donald Keyhoe
Dorothy Kilner
Dougan Clark
Douglas Fairbanks
E. Nesbit
E. P. Roe
E. Phillips Oppenheim
E. S. Brooks
Earl Barnes
Edgar Rice Burroughs
Edith Van Dyne
Edith Wharton

Edward Everett Hale
Edward J. O'Biren
Edward S. Ellis
Edwin L. Arnold
Eleanor Atkins
Eleanor Hallowell Abbott
Eliot Gregory
Elizabeth Gaskell
Elizabeth McCracken
Elizabeth Von Arnim
Ellem Key
Emerson Hough
Emilie F. Carlen
Emily Bronte
Emily Dickinson
Enid Bagnold
Enilor Macartney Lane
Erasmus W. Jones
Ernie Howard Pie
Ethel May Dell
Ethel Turner
Ethel Watts Mumford
Eugene Sue
Eugenie Foa
Eugene Wood
Eustace Hale Ball
Evelyn Everett-green
Everard Cotes
F. H. Cheley
F. J. Cross
F. Marion Crawford
Fannie E. Newberry
Federick Austin Ogg
Ferdinand Ossendowski
Fergus Hume
Florence A. Kilpatrick
Fremont B. Deering
Francis Bacon
Francis Darwin
Frances Hodgson Burnett
Frances Parkinson Keyes
Frank Gee Patchin
Frank Harris
Frank Jewett Mather
Frank L. Packard
Frank V. Webster
Frederic Stewart Isham
Frederick Trevor Hill
Frederick Winslow Taylor

Friedrich Kerst
Friedrich Nietzsche
Fyodor Dostoyevsky
G.A. Henty
G.K. Chesterton
Gabrielle E. Jackson
Garrett P. Serviss
Gaston Leroux
George A. Warren
George Ade
Geroge Bernard Shaw
George Cary Eggleston
George Durston
George Ebers
George Eliot
George Gissing
George MacDonald
George Meredith
George Orwell
George Sylvester Viereck
George Tucker
George W. Cable
George Wharton James
Gertrude Atherton
Gordon Casserly
Grace E. King
Grace Gallatin
Grace Greenwood
Grant Allen
Guillermo A. Sherwell
Gulielma Zollinger
Gustav Flaubert
H. A. Cody
H. B. Irving
H.C. Bailey
H. G. Wells
H. H. Munro
H. Irving Hancock
H. R. Naylor
H. Rider Haggard
H. W. C. Davis
Haldeman Julius
Hall Caine
Hamilton Wright Mabie
Hans Christian Andersen
Harold Avery
Harold McGrath
Harriet Beecher Stowe
Harry Castlemon
Harry Coghill
Harry Houidini

Hayden Carruth
Helent Hunt Jackson
Helen Nicolay
Hendrik Conscience
Hendy David Thoreau
Henri Barbusse
Henrik Ibsen
Henry Adams
Henry Ford
Henry Frost
Henry James
Henry Jones Ford
Henry Seton Merriman
Henry W Longfellow
Herbert A. Giles
Herbert Carter
Herbert N. Casson
Herman Hesse
Hildegard G. Frey
Homer
Honore De Balzac
Horace B. Day
Horace Walpole
Horatio Alger Jr.
Howard Pyle
Howard R. Garis
Hugh Lofting
Hugh Walpole
Humphry Ward
Ian Maclaren
Inez Haynes Gillmore
Irving Bacheller
Isabel Cecilia Williams
Isabel Hornibrook
Israel Abrahams
Ivan Turgenev
J.G.Austin
J. Henri Fabre
J. M. Barrie
J. M. Walsh
J. Macdonald Oxley
J. R. Miller
J. S. Fletcher
J. S. Knowles
J. Storer Clouston
J. W. Duffield
Jack London
Jacob Abbott
James Allen
James Andrews
James Baldwin

James Branch Cabell
James DeMille
James Joyce
James Lane Allen
James Lane Allen
James Oliver Curwood
James Oppenheim
James Otis
James R. Driscoll
Jane Abbott
Jane Austen
Jane L. Stewart
Janet Aldridge
Jens Peter Jacobsen
Jerome K. Jerome
Jessie Graham Flower
John Buchan
John Burroughs
John Cournos
John F. Kennedy
John Gay
John Glasworthy
John Habberton
John Joy Bell
John Kendrick Bangs
John Milton
John Philip Sousa
John Taintor Foote
Jonas Lauritz Idemil Lie
Jonathan Swift
Joseph A. Altsheler
Joseph Carey
Joseph Conrad
Joseph E. Badger Jr
Joseph Hergesheimer
Joseph Jacobs
Jules Vernes
Julian Hawthrone
Julie A Lippmann
Justin Huntly McCarthy
Kakuzo Okakura
Karle Wilson Baker
Kate Chopin
Kenneth Grahame
Kenneth McGaffey
Kate Langley Bosher
Kate Langley Bosher
Katherine Cecil Thurston
Katherine Stokes
L. A. Abbot
L. T. Meade

L. Frank Baum
Latta Griswold
Laura Dent Crane
Laura Lee Hope
Laurence Housman
Lawrence Beasley
Leo Tolstoy
Leonid Andreyev
Lewis Carroll
Lewis Sperry Chafer
Lilian Bell
Lloyd Osbourne
Louis Hughes
Louis Joseph Vance
Louis Tracy
Louisa May Alcott
Lucy Fitch Perkins
Lucy Maud Montgomery
Luther Benson
Lydia Miller Middleton
Lyndon Orr
M. Corvus
M. H. Adams
Margaret E. Sangster
Margret Howth
Margaret Vandercook
Margaret W. Hungerford
Margret Penrose
Maria Edgeworth
Maria Thompson Daviess
Mariano Azuela
Marion Polk Angellotti
Mark Overton
Mark Twain
Mary Austin
Mary Catherine Crowley
Mary Cole
Mary Hastings Bradley
Mary Roberts Rinehart
Mary Rowlandson
M. Wollstonecraft Shelley
Maud Lindsay
Max Beerbohm
Myra Kelly
Nathaniel Hawthrone
Nicolo Machiavelli
O. F. Walton
Oscar Wilde

Owen Johnson
P.G. Wodehouse
Paul and Mabel Thorne
Paul G. Tomlinson
Paul Severing
Percy Brebner
Percy Keese Fitzhugh
Peter B. Kyne
Plato
Quincy Allen
R. Derby Holmes
R. L. Stevenson
R. S. Ball
Rabindranath Tagore
Rahul Alvares
Ralph Bonehill
Ralph Henry Barbour
Ralph Victor
Ralph Waldo Emmerson
Rene Descartes
Ray Cummings
Rex Beach
Rex E. Beach
Richard Harding Davis
Richard Jefferies
Richard Le Gallienne
Robert Barr
Robert Frost
Robert Gordon Anderson
Robert L. Drake
Robert Lansing
Robert Lynd
Robert Michael Ballantyne
Robert W. Chambers
Rosa Nouchette Carey
Rudyard Kipling
Saint Augustine
Samuel B. Allison
Samuel Hopkins Adams
Sarah Bernhardt
Sarah C. Hallowell
Selma Lagerlof
Sherwood Anderson
Sigmund Freud
Standish O'Grady
Stanley Weyman
Stella Benson
Stella M. Francis

Stephen Crane
Stewart Edward White
Stijn Streuvels
Swami Abhedananda
Swami Parmananda
T. S. Ackland
T. S. Arthur
The Princess Der Ling
Thomas A. Janvier
Thomas A Kempis
Thomas Anderton
Thomas Bailey Aldrich
Thomas Bulfinch
Thomas De Quincey
Thomas Dixon
Thomas H. Huxley
Thomas Hardy
Thomas More
Thornton W. Burgess
U. S. Grant
Upton Sinclair
Valentine Williams
Various Authors
Vaughan Kester
Victor Appleton
Victor G. Durham
Victoria Cross
Virginia Woolf
Wadsworth Camp
Walter Camp
Walter Scott
Washington Irving
Wilbur Lawton
Wilkie Collins
Willa Cather
Willard F. Baker
William Dean Howells
William le Queux
W. Makepeace Thackeray
William W. Walter
William Shakespeare
Winston Churchill
Yei Theodora Ozaki
Yogi Ramacharaka
Young E. Allison
Zane Grey